Applying Ṣarf

Book 2: al-Thulāthī al-Mazīd Fīh

Shaykh Abdullah Ayaz Mullanee

Shaykha Aamina Jamil

Shaykha Raabia Ghasemi

Credits

Authors:
Shaykha Aamina Jamil
Shaykh Abdullah Ayaz Mullanee
Shaykha Raabia Ghasemi

Editors:
Yasmin Khatau
Shaykh Olinoor Mia
Shameela Shaikh

Formatting:

Shameela Shaikh
Tanzeela Shaikh

Published by Lubab Academy
Lubab Academy conducts live classes online on weekend mornings. These classes are aimed for the average adult Muslim and include Arabic, Qurʾān recitation, fundamental and Tafsīr. For more information, see
www.lubabacademy.com

Foreword

We are finishing this book during the last ten days of Ramadan. Last year, we had the opportunity to publish and teach Applying Ṣarf Volume 1 to our students, and we have learned so much from that experience.

The Applying Sarf series seeks to unite the theoretical rules of Ṣarf with practical examples based on Qurʾān and Ḥadīth. In volume 2, students are introduced to al-Thulāthī al-Mazīd Fīh verbs and are then provided with empty Ṣarf Ṣaghīr and Ṣarf Kabīr charts to practice the patterns. Next, they are provided with fifteen Arabic examples mostly based on the Qurʾān and Ḥadīth. This is followed by an exercise testing the students' ability to form the verb on their own. Every few chapters, the book also provides review exercises covering all the content that has been covered thus far.

It should be noted that this book is purely an Arabic grammar book. Many of the Aḥādīth are weak, and many of the theoretical grammar exercises sound odd when translated into English. Teachers should look into the situations and commentaries of the verses and Aḥādīth provided in order to give a more comprehensive and interesting lesson in class.

An appendix of rare patterns has been included at the end of this book which learners may choose to skip.

We have also taken the time to answer the questions of this book ourselves. This has allowed us to experience the book in the way that the learners will experience it. It also brought to light many mistakes and oddities that sounded fine theoretically but practically did not make sense. We also have reworded some of the Arabic texts to make it simpler and more comprehensive for the beginner students working on this book.The next volume and final volume planned in the series will deal with al-Fiʿl al-Rubāʿī and irregular verbs (al-Taʿlīlāt).

We pray that may Allah make this volume and the entire series a means of barakah for its authors, editors, supporters, learners, and teachers alike! May Allah bless you for purchasing this book, and we hope you are ready for a deep dive into the ocean of Ṣarf!

Please keep us in your Duʿās,

Aamina Jamil, Abdullah Ayaz Mullanee & Raabia Ghasemi

May 6th, 2021
Ramadan 23, 1442

Table of Contents

Review

Words

<u>In Arabic, words are of three types:</u>

1) **al-Fiʻl (الفِعْل):** A word which provides a definite meaning and is associated with one of the three tenses. These are the equivalent of verbs in English.
   Example: ضَرَبَ: He hit.

   يَفْتَحُ: He opens or will open.

2) **al-Ism (الإِسْم):** A word which provides a definite meaning and is not associated with one of the three tenses. These are the equivalent of nouns in English.
   Example: قَلَمٌ: a pen

   الْكِتَابُ: the book

3) **al-Ḥarf (الْحَرْف):** A word which does not provide a definite meaning, and it cannot become a substantial part of a sentence without joining another word with it.
   Example: مِنْ: from

According to the scholars of ṣarf, fiʻls are the root of all words, and they will be the focus of this book.

al-Māḍī, al-Muḍāriʿ and al-Amr

Fiʿls are of three types:

1) **al-Māḍī** (الْمَاضِي): A fiʿl which relays a meaning that occurred in the past tense.
   Example: نَصَرَ: He helped.

2) **al-Muḍāriʿ** (الْمُضَارِع): A fiʿl which relays a meaning that occurred in the present or future tense.
   Example: يَنْصُرُ: He helps or will help.

3) **al-Amr** (الْأَمْر): A fiʿl through which an action is desired from the doer in the future tense. This can be understood as a command or an imperative.
   Example: أُنْصُرْ: Help!

al-Muthbat and al-Manfī

1) **al-Muthbat** (الْمُثْبَت): A fiʿl which indicates upon its occurrence. In other words, this is a positive fiʿl.
   Example: جَلَسَ: He sat.

2) **al-Manfī** (الْمَنْفِي): A fiʿl which indicates upon the absence of its occurrence. In other words, this is a negative fiʿl.
   Example: مَا ضَرَبَ: He did not hit.

Note: In the making of a manfī fiʾl, we generally add مَا in front of māḍī fiʿls and لَا in front of muḍāriʿ fiʿls.
Example: مَا ضَرَبَ: He did not hit.

لَا يَضْرِبُ: He does not hit or will not hit.

al-Maʿrūf and al-Majhūl

1) **al-Maʿrūf (الْمَعْرُوف):** A fiʿl which is associated with its doer. This is known as active voice in English.

   Example: سَمِعَ: He heard.

   لَا تَجْلِسُ: She does not sit or will not sit.

2) **al-Majhūl (الْمَجْهُول):** A fiʿl which is associated with its object. This is known as passive voice in English.

   Example: ضُرِبَ: He was hit.

   يُسْمَعُ: He is heard or will be heard.

al-Thulāthī and al-Rubāʿī

<u>When considering the root letters, fiʿls have four types:</u>

1) **al-Thulāthī al-Mujarrad (الثُّلَاثِيُّ الْمُجَرَّدُ):** A fiʿl which is comprised of three root letters, and there are no additional letters in its māḍī form besides them.

   Example: خَلَقَ: He created.

2) **al-Thulāthī al-Mazīd Fīh (الثُّلَاثِيُّ الْمَزِيدُ فِيهِ):** A fiʿl which is comprised of three root letters, and there are additional letters joined to them in its māḍī form.

   Example: أَرْسَلَ: He sent.

3) **al-Rubāʿī al-Mujarrad (الرُّبَاعِيُّ الْمُجَرَّدُ):** A fiʿl which is comprised of four root letters, and there are no additional letters in its māḍī form besides them.

   Example: بَعْثَرَ: He scattered (something else).

4) **al-Rubāʿī al-Mazīd Fīh (الرُّبَاعِيُّ الْمَزِيدُ فِيهِ):** A fiʿl which comprises of four root letters, and there are additional letters joined to them in its māḍī form.

   Example: تَبَعْثَرَ: He became scattered.

al-Lāzim and al-Mutaʿaddī

When considering whether a fiʿl needs an object (المفعول به), fiʿls are of two types:

1) al-Lāzim (الْلَازِم): A fiʿl which does not have an object. In English, these are known as intransitive verbs.
   Example: مَاتَ: He died.

2) al-Mutaʿaddī (الْمُتَعَدِّي): A fiʿl which can have an object. In English, these are known as transitive verbs.
   Example: ضَرَبَ عَلِيٌّ زَيْدًا: ʿAlī hit Zayd.

Note: If a fiʿl can only connect to an object with the help of a ḥarf, that verb will still be considered al-Lāzim.

Example: جلستُ على الكرسي: I sat on the chair. In this example, جلس is al-Lāzim because it is unable to connect to its object, الكرسي, without the addition of the ḥarf 'على'.

Detailed Discussion

Chapter 1: al-Thulāthī al-Mazīd Fīh

Unit 1: Introduction - Definition of al-Thulāthī al-Mazīd Fīh and Its Patterns

al-Thulāthī al-Mazīd Fīh (الثُّلَاثِيُّ الْمَزِيدُ فِيهِ): A fiʿl which is comprised of three root letters, and there are additional letters joined to them in its Māḍī form. Example: أَرْسَلَ: He sent.

There are 14 patterns of al-Thulāthī al-Mazīd Fīh. 9 of them are commonly used patterns, while the remaining 5 are rarely used.

The 9 most commonly used patterns are:

بَاب التَّفْعِيل	فَعَّلَ يُفَعِّلُ – تَفْعِيلًا[1]	(2
بَاب الْمُفَاعَلَة	فَاعَلَ يُفَاعِلُ – مُفَاعَلَةً	(3
بَاب الْإِفْعَال	أَفْعَلَ يُفْعِلُ – إِفْعَالًا	(4
بَاب التَّفَعُّل	تَفَعَّلَ يَتَفَعَّلُ – تَفَعُّلًا	(5
بَاب التَّفَاعُل	تَفَاعَلَ يَتَفَاعَلُ – تَفَاعُلًا	(6
بَاب الِانْفِعَال	انْفَعَلَ يَنْفَعِلُ – انْفِعَالًا	(7
بَاب الِافْتِعَال	افْتَعَلَ يَفْتَعِلُ – افْتِعَالًا	(8
بَاب الِافْعِلَال	افْعَلَّ يَفْعَلُّ – افْعِلَالًا	(9
بَاب الِاسْتِفْعَال	اِسْتَفْعَلَ يَسْتَفْعِلُ – اسْتِفْعَالًا	(10

---

[1] The numbering starts from two because pattern one is the Thulāthī Mujarrad pattern which was taught in Applying Sarf 1.

Unit 2: The Second Pattern – التفعيل

This pattern is identified by the number II in the Hans Wehr dictionary. It often turns Lāzim verbs into Mutaʿaddī.

مُفَعَّلٌ	تَفْعِيلًا	يُفَعِّلُ	فَعَّلَ
الاسم الفاعل	المصدر	المضارع المعروف	الماضي المعروف
مُفَعَّلٌ	تَفْعِيلًا	يُفَعَّلُ	فُعِّلَ
الاسم المفعول	المصدر	المضارع المجهول	الماضي المجهول
	لَا تُفَعِّلْ		فَعِّلْ
	النهي		الأمر

Exercises

Question 1: Please fill in the following:

a)

			كَذَّبَ
الاسم الفاعل	المصدر	المضارع المعروف	الماضي المعروف
الاسم المفعول	المصدر	المضارع المجهول	الماضي المجهول
		النهي	الأمر

b)

			قَدَّمَ
الاسم الفاعل	المصدر	المضارع المعروف	الماضي المعروف
الاسم المفعول	المصدر	المضارع المجهول	الماضي المجهول
		النهي	الأمر

c)

			عَظَّمَ
الاسم الفاعل	المصدر	المضارع المعروف	الماضي المعروف
الاسم المفعول	المصدر	المضارع المجهول	الماضي المجهول
		النهي	الأمر

d)

			عَجَّلَ
الاسم الفاعل	المصدر	المضارع المعروف	الماضي المعروف
الاسم المفعول	المصدر	المضارع المجهول	الماضي المجهول
		النهي	الأمر

e)

			بَلَّغَ
الاسم الفاعل	المصدر	المضارع المعروف	الماضي المعروف
الاسم المفعول	المصدر	المضارع المجهول	الماضي المجهول
		النهي	الأمر

f)

			ذَكَّرَ
الاسم الفاعل	المصدر	المضارع المعروف	الماضي المعروف
الاسم المفعول	المصدر	المضارع المجهول	الماضي المجهول
		النهي	الأمر

Question 2: Please fill in the following:

al-Tafʿīl al-Fiʿl al-Māḍī al-Muthbat al-Maʿrūf		
He denied	Singular, male, third person	كَذَّبَ
	Dual, male, third person	
	Plural, male, third person	
	Singular, female, third person	
	Dual, female, third person	
	Plural, female, third person	
	Singular, male, second person	
	Dual, male, second person	
	Plural, male, second person	
	Singular, female, second person	
	Dual, female, second person	
	Plural, female second person	
	Singular, first person	
	Plural, first person	

al-Tafʿīl al-Fiʿl al-Muḍāriʿ al-Muthbat al-Maʿrūf		
	Singular, male, third person	يُبَلِّغُ
	Dual, male, third person	
	Plural, male, third person	
	Singular, female, third person	
	Dual, female, third person	
	Plural, female, third person	
	Singular, male, second person	
	Dual, male, second person	
	Plural, male, second person	
	Singular, female, second person	
	Dual, female, second person	
	Plural, female second person	
	Singular, first person	
	Plural, first person	

al-Tafʿīl al-Fiʿl al-Muḍāriʿ al-Manfī al-Majhūl		
	Singular, male, third person	لَا يُذَكَّرُ
	Dual, male, third person	
	Plural, male, third person	
	Singular, female, third person	
	Dual, female, third person	
	Plural, female, third person	
	Singular, male, second person	
	Dual, male, second person	
	Plural, male, second person	
	Singular, female, second person	
	Dual, female, second person	
	Plural, female second person	
	Singular, first person	
	Plural, first person	

al-Tafʿīl al-Fiʿl al-Muḍāriʿ al-Manfī al-Majhūl

al-Tafʿīl	al-Fiʿl al-Amr al-Maʿrūf	
	Singular, male, third person	لِيُعَظِّمْ
	Dual, male, third person	
	Plural, male, third person	
	Singular, female, third person	
	Dual, female, third person	
	Plural, female, third person	
	Singular, male, second person	
	Dual, male, second person	
	Plural, male, second person	
	Singular, female, second person	
	Dual, female, second person	
	Plural, female second person	
	Singular, first person	
	Plural, first person	

Question 3: Translate the following into English:

هُوَ الَّذِي يُصَوِّرُكُمْ فِي الْأَرْحَامِ كَيْفَ يَشَاءُ	(1
زُيِّنَ لِلنَّاسِ حُبُّ الشَّهَوَاتِ مِنَ النِّسَاءِ وَالْبَنِينَ وَالْقَنَاطِيرِ الْمُقَنْطَرَةِ مِنَ الذَّهَبِ وَالْفِضَّةِ وَالْخَيْلِ الْمُسَوَّمَةِ وَالْأَنْعَامِ وَالْحَرْثِ	(2
بَشِّرْهُمْ بِعَذَابٍ أَلِيمٍ	(3
سَيُطَوَّقُونَ مَا بَخِلُوا بِهِ يَوْمَ الْقِيَامَةِ	(4
يَا أَيُّهَا الَّذِينَ آمَنُوا لَا تُقَدِّمُوا بَيْنَ يَدَيِ اللهِ وَرَسُولِهِ	(5

6)	قُلْ أَتُعَلِّمُونَ اللهَ بِدِينِكُمْ
7)	كَلَّا تَبَّرْنَا تَتْبِيرًا
8)	إِنْ نَشَأْ نُنَزِّلْ عَلَيْهِمْ مِنَ السَّمَاءِ آيَةً فَظَلَّتْ أَعْنَاقُهُمْ لَهَا خَاضِعِينَ
9)	قَالَ أَلَمْ نُرَبِّكَ فِينَا وَلِيدًا وَلَبِثْتَ فِينَا مِنْ عُمُرِكَ سِنِينَ
10)	جَهَّزَهُمْ بِجَهَازِهِمْ

(11	لَا تُبَذِّرْ تَبْذِيرًا
(12	حَرِّضِ الْمُؤْمِنِينَ
(13	وَلَوْ يُعَجِّلُ اللهُ لِلنَّاسِ الشَّرَّ
(14	وَلَا تُصَعِّرْ خَدَّكَ لِلنَّاسِ
(15	لَقَدْ صَبَّحَهُمْ بُكْرَةً عَذَابٌ

Question 4: Fill out the following chart:

	Masdar	Verb Form		Arabic
1.	تقطيع	Maḍī Muthbat Maʿrūf	Singular, female, third person	
	Translation			
2.	تحذير	Nahī Majhūl	Plural, male, first person	
	Translation			
3.	تفريغ	Ism Fāʿil	Singular, female	
	Translation			
4.	ترتيل	Muḍāriʿ Manfī Maʿrūf	Plural, first person	
	Translation			
5.	تدريس	Amr Majhūl	Dual, female, third person	
	Translation			

	Masdar	Verb Form		Arabic
6.	تنزيل	Māḍī Manfī Majhūl	Singular, first person	
	Translation			
7.	تشخيص	Muḍāriᶜ Manfī Majhūl	Dual, male, second person	
	Translation			
8.	تصنيف	Muḍhāriᶜ Muthbat Maᶜrūf	Plural, female, third person	
	Translation			
9.	تعليم	Ism Mafᶜūl	Plural, male	
	Translation			
10.	تجليد	Māḍī Manfī Maᶜrūf	Dual, male, third person	
	Translation			

Masdar	Verb Form		Arabic
11.			مُقَدَّرَانِ
Translation			
12.			نُمَجِّدُ
Translation			
13.			صَدَّقْ
Translation			
14.			سُخِّرْتُمَا
Translation			
15.			لَا تُبَشِّرْنَ
Translation			

Unit 3: The Third Pattern – المفاعلة

This pattern is identified by the number III in the Hans Wehr dictionary. This pattern is often used to turn al-Fiʿl al-Lāzim into al-Fiʿl al-Mutaʿaddī.

مُفَاعِلٌ	مُفَاعَلَةً وَ فِعَالًا	يُفَاعِلُ	فَاعَلَ
الاسم الفاعل	المصدر	المضارع المعروف	الماضي المعروف
مُفَاعَلٌ	مُفَاعَلَةً وَ فِعَالًا	يُفَاعَلُ	فُوعِلَ
الاسم المفعول	المصدر	المضارع المجهول	الماضي المجهول
		لَا تُفَاعِلْ	فَاعِلْ
		النهي	الأمر

Exercises

Question 1: Please fill in the following:

a)

			قَاتَلَ
الاسم الفاعل	المصدر	المضارع المعروف	الماضي المعروف
الاسم المفعول	المصدر	المضارع المجهول	الماضي المجهول
		النهي	الأمر

b)

			خَادَعَ
الاسم الفاعل	المصدر	المضارع المعروف	الماضي المعروف
الاسم المفعول	المصدر	المضارع المجهول	الماضي المجهول
		النهي	الأمر

c)

			عَاقَبَ
الاسم الفاعل	المصدر	المضارع المعروف	الماضي المعروف
الاسم المفعول	المصدر	المضارع المجهول	الماضي المجهول
		النهي	الأمر

d)

			لَازَمَ
الاسم الفاعل	المصدر	المضارع المعروف	الماضي المعروف
الاسم المفعول	المصدر	المضارع المجهول	الماضي المجهول
		النهي	الأمر

e)

			شَارَكَ
الاسم الفاعل	المصدر	المضارع المعروف	الماضي المعروف
الاسم المفعول	المصدر	المضارع المجهول	الماضي المجهول
		النهي	الأمر

f)

			رَاقَبَ
الاسم الفاعل	المصدر	المضارع المعروف	الماضي المعروف
الاسم المفعول	المصدر	المضارع المجهول	الماضي المجهول
		النهي	الأمر

Question 2: Please fill in the following:

al-Mufāʿala al-Fiʿl al-Māḍī al-Manfī al-Maʿrūf		
	Singular, male, third person	ما شارَكَ
	Dual, male, third person	
	Plural, male, third person	
	Singular, female, third person	
	Dual, female, third person	
	Plural, female, third person	
	Singular, male, second person	
	Dual, male, second person	
	Plural, male, second person	
	Singular, female, second person	
	Dual, female, second person	
	Plural, female second person	
	Singular, first person	
	Plural, first person	

al-Mufāʿala al-Fiʿl al-Muḍāriʿ al-Muthbat al-Majhūl		
	Singular, male, third person	يُخَادَعُ
	Dual, male, third person	
	Plural, male, third person	
	Singular, female, third person	
	Dual, female, third person	
	Plural, female, third person	
	Singular, male, second person	
	Dual, male, second person	
	Plural, male, second person	
	Singular, female, second person	
	Dual, female, second person	
	Plural, female second person	
	Singular, first person	
	Plural, first person	

al-Mufāʿala al-Fiʿl al-Muḍāriʿ al-Manfī al-Majhūl		
	Singular, male, third person	لَا يُعَاقَبُ
	Dual, male, third person	
	Plural, male, third person	
	Singular, female, third person	
	Dual, female, third person	
	Plural, female, third person	
	Singular, male, second person	
	Dual, male, second person	
	Plural, male, second person	
	Singular, female, second person	
	Dual, female, second person	
	Plural, female second person	
	Singular, first person	
	Plural, first person	

al-Mufāʿala al-Fiʿl al-Nahī al-Maʿrūf		
	Singular, male, third person	لَا يُلَازِمْ
	Dual, male, third person	
	Plural, male, third person	
	Singular, female, third person	
	Dual, female, third person	
	Plural, female, third person	
	Singular, male, second person	
	Dual, male, second person	
	Plural, male, second person	
	Singular, female, second person	
	Dual, female, second person	
	Plural, female second person	
	Singular, first person	
	Plural, first person	

Question 3: Translate the following into English:

يُوقَدُ مِنْ شَجَرَةٍ مُبَارَكَةٍ زَيْتُونَةٍ	(1
فَقَالُوا رَبَّنَا بَاعِدْ بَيْنَ أَسْفَارِنَا	(2
قَدْ سَمِعَ اللهُ قَوْلَ الَّتِي تُجَادِلُكَ فِي زَوْجِهَا	(3
فَسَوْفَ يُحَاسَبُ حِسَابًا يَسِيرًا	(4
إِنَّ الْمُنَافِقِينَ يُخَادِعُونَ اللهَ وَهُوَ خَادِعُهُمْ	(5

(6	لَا يَمْلِكُونَ مِنْهُ خِطَابًا
	_____
(7	لَا تُخَاطِبْنِي فِي الَّذِينَ ظَلَمُوا
	_____
(8	لَا صَلَاةَ بِحَضْرَةِ الطَّعَامِ، وَلَا هُوَ يُدَافِعُهُ الْأَخْبَثَانِ
	_____
	_____
(9	وَهُزِّي إِلَيْكِ بِجِذْعِ النَّخْلَةِ تُسَاقِطْ عَلَيْكِ رُطَبًا جَنِيًّا
	_____
	_____
(10	وَشَارَكْهُمْ فِي الْأَمْوَالِ وَالْأَوْلَادِ
	_____

قَالَ إِنْ سَأَلْتُكَ عَنْ شَيْءٍ بَعْدَهَا فَلَا تُصَاحِبْنِي	(11
مَنْ ذَا الَّذِي يُقْرِضُ اللَّهَ قَرْضًا حَسَنًا فَيُضَاعِفَهُ لَهُ أَضْعَافًا كَثِيرَةً	(12
وَإِنْ عَاقَبْتُمْ فَعَاقِبُوا بِمِثْلِ مَا عُوقِبْتُمْ بِهِ	(13
أَوَكُلَّمَا عَاهَدُوا عَهْدًا نَبَذَهُ فَرِيقٌ مِنْهُمْ	(14
فَإِذَا بَلَغْنَ أَجَلَهُنَّ فَأَمْسِكُوهُنَّ بِمَعْرُوفٍ أَوْ فَارِقُوهُنَّ بِمَعْرُوفٍ	(15

Question 4: Fill out the following chart:

	Masdar	Verb Form		Arabic
1.	مطالعة	Muḍāriʿ Muthbat Maʿrūf	Dual, male, second person	
	Translation			
2.	مسارعة	Ism Fāʿil	Plural, female	
	Translation			
3.	مضاربة	Māḍī Manfī Maʿrūf	Plural, male, third person	
	Translation			
4.	مطالبة	Ism Mafʿūl	Dual, male	
	Translation			
5.	مراقبة	Muḍāriʿ Muthbat Majhūl	Dual, male, second person	
	Translation			

	Masdar	Verb Form		Arabic
6.	مرافقة	Amr Maʿrūf	Plural, first person	
	Translation			
7.	مخالفة	Māḍī Muthbat Majhūl	Singular, male, second person	
	Translation			
8.	مشاغلة	Nahī Maʿrūf	Dual, female, third person	
	Translation			
9.	مشاحنة	Ism Fāʿil	Dual, male	
	Translation			
10.	مشاهدة	Māḍī Manfī Majhūl	Singular, female, third person	
	Translation			

	Masdar	Verb Form		Arabic
11.				يُخَابِرُونَ
	Translation			
12.				عَانِقِيْ
	Translation			
13.				لَا نُجَادِلْ
	Translation			
14.				مُسَاعِدٌ
	Translation			
15.				لِأُتَابَعْ
	Translation			

Unit 4: The Fourth Pattern – الإفعال

This pattern is identified by the number IV in the Hans Wehr dictionary. This pattern is generally used to turn al-Fiʿl al-Lāzim into al-Fiʿl al-Mutaʿaddī.

It should be noted that the first *hamza* in the beginning of this pattern is not a *hamza al-waṣl*.

مُفْعِلٌ	إفْعَالًا	يُفْعِلُ	أَفْعَلَ
الاسم الفاعل	المصدر	المضارع المعروف	الماضي المعروف
مُفْعَلٌ	إفْعَالًا	يُفْعَلُ	أُفْعِلَ
الاسم المفعول	المصدر	المضارع المجهول	الماضي المجهول
	لَا تُفْعِلْ		أَفْعِلْ
	النهي		الأمر

Exercises

Question 1: Please fill in the following:

a)

			أَكْرَمَ
الاسم الفاعل	المصدر	المضارع المعروف	الماضي المعروف
الاسم المفعول	المصدر	المضارع المجهول	الماضي المجهول
		النهي	الأمر

b)

			أَسْلَمَ
الاسم الفاعل	المصدر	المضارع المعروف	الماضي المعروف
الاسم المفعول	المصدر	المضارع المجهول	الماضي المجهول
		النهي	الأمر

c)

			أَعْلَنَ
الاسم الفاعل	المصدر	المضارع المعروف	الماضي المعروف
الاسم المفعول	المصدر	المضارع المجهول	الماضي المجهول
		النهي	الأمر

d)

الاسم الفاعل	المصدر	المضارع المعروف	أَذْهَبَ
			الماضي المعروف
الاسم المفعول	المصدر	المضارع المجهول	
			الماضي المجهول
		النهي	الأمر

e)

الاسم الفاعل	المصدر	المضارع المعروف	أَطْعَمَ
			الماضي المعروف
الاسم المفعول	المصدر	المضارع المجهول	
			الماضي المجهول
		النهي	الأمر

f)

الاسم الفاعل	المصدر	المضارع المعروف	أَخْرَجَ
			الماضي المعروف
الاسم المفعول	المصدر	المضارع المجهول	
			الماضي المجهول
		النهي	الأمر

Question 2: Please fill in the following:

	al-Ifʿāl al-Fiʿl al-Māḍī al-Manfī al-Maʿrūf	
	Singular, male, third person	ما أَصْلَحَ
	Dual, male, third person	
	Plural, male, third person	
	Singular, female, third person	
	Dual, female, third person	
	Plural, female, third person	
	Singular, male, second person	
	Dual, male, second person	
	Plural, male, second person	
	Singular, female, second person	
	Dual, female, second person	
	Plural, female second person	
	Singular, first person	
	Plural, first person	

	al-Ifʿāl al-Fiʿl al-Muḍāriʿ al-Manfī al-Maʿrūf	
	Singular, male, third person	لَا يُعْلِنُ
	Dual, male, third person	
	Plural, male, third person	
	Singular, female, third person	
	Dual, female, third person	
	Plural, female, third person	
	Singular, male, second person	
	Dual, male, second person	
	Plural, male, second person	
	Singular, female, second person	
	Dual, female, second person	
	Plural, female second person	
	Singular, first person	
	Plural, first person	

al-Ifʿāl al-Fiʿl al-Muḍāriʿ al-Muthbat al-Majhūl		
	Singular, male, third person	يُخْرَجُ
	Dual, male, third person	
	Plural, male, third person	
	Singular, female, third person	
	Dual, female, third person	
	Plural, female, third person	
	Singular, male, second person	
	Dual, male, second person	
	Plural, male, second person	
	Singular, female, second person	
	Dual, female, second person	
	Plural, female second person	
	Singular, first person	
	Plural, first person	

al-Ifʿāl al-Fiʿl al-Nahī al-Majhūl

	Singular, male, third person	لَا يُذْهَبْ
	Dual, male, third person	
	Plural, male, third person	
	Singular, female, third person	
	Dual, female, third person	
	Plural, female, third person	
	Singular, male, second person	
	Dual, male, second person	
	Plural, male, second person	
	Singular, female, second person	
	Dual, female, second person	
	Plural, female second person	
	Singular, first person	
	Plural, first person	

Question 3: Translate the following into English:

(1	لَا يُصَدَّعُونَ عَنْهَا وَلَا يُنْزِفُونَ
(2	إِنَّا أَنْشَأْنَاهُنَّ إِنْشَاءً
(3	مِنْهُ آيَاتٌ مُحْكَمَاتٌ
(4	ثَلَاثٌ لَا يُغِلُّ عَلَيْهِنَّ قَلْبُ مُسْلِمٍ، إِخْلَاصُ الْعَمَلِ لِلَّهِ، وَمُنَاصَحَةُ وُلَاةِ الْأَمْرِ، وَلُزُومُ الْجَمَاعَةِ
(5	غُفِرَ لَكَ بِإِخْلَاصِكَ قَوْلَ: لَا إِلَهَ إِلا اللهُ

6)	مَا يُمْسِكُ الطَّيْرَ إِلَّا الرَّحْمَٰنُ
7)	بَلْ عَجِبُوا أَنْ جَاءَهُمْ مُنْذِرٌ مِنْهُمْ
8)	أَنْبَتْنَا فِي الْأَرْضِ مِنْ كُلِّ زَوْجٍ كَرِيمٍ
9)	عَسَىٰ رَبُّنَا أَنْ يُبْدِلَنَا خَيْرًا مِنْهَا إِنَّا إِلَىٰ رَبِّنَا رَاغِبُونَ
10	وَإِرْشَادُكَ الرَّجُلَ فِي أَرْضِ الضَّلَالِ لَكَ صَدَقَةٌ

وَآتَيْنَا ثَمُودَ النَّاقَةَ مُبْصِرَةً	(11
أَبُو شُعَيْبٍ أَبْصَرَ فِي وَجْهِ النَّبِيِّ صَلَّى اللهُ عَلَيْهِ وَسَلَّمَ الْجُوعَ	(12
قَالَ اللهُ لِإِبْرَاهِيمَ أَسْلِمْ رَبُّهُ قَالَ أَسْلَمْتُ لِرَبِّ الْعَالَمِينَ	(13
يَا أَرْضُ ابْلَعِي مَاءَكِ وَيَا سَمَاءُ أَقْلِعِي	(14
قَالَ يَا قَوْمِ لَقَدْ أَبْلَغْتُكُمْ رِسَالَةَ رَبِّي وَنَصَحْتُ لَكُمْ	(15

Question 4: Fill out the following chart:

	Masdar	Verb Form		Arabic
1.	إكرام	Māḍī Manfī Maʿrūf	Dual, male	
	Translation			
2.	إفلاس	Amr Maʿrūf	Singular, female, third person	
	Translation			
3.	إلهام	Ism Mafʿūl	Plural, male	
	Translation			
4.	إفلاح	Muḍāriʿ Manfī Majhūl	Plural, female	
	Translation			
5.	إقبال	Māḍī Muthbat Majhūl	Plural, first person	
	Translation			

	Masdar	Verb Form		Arabic
6.	إنعام	Nahī Maʿrūf	Singular, first person	
	Translation			
7.	إفهام	Ism Fāʿil	Singular, male	
	Translation			
8.	إفراح	Māḍī Manfī Majhūl	Plural, male, third person	
	Translation			
9.	إكمال	Muḍāriʿ Muthbat Maʿrūf	Singular, female, second person	
	Translation			
10.				أَرْشَدْنَ
	Translation			

	Masdar	Verb Form		Arabic
11.				لَا تُغْلِقَا
	Translation			
12.				مُسْلِمَةٌ
	Translation			
13.				لِيُمْسِكَا
	Translation			
14.				لَا أُثْبَتُ
	Translation			
15.				مُفْطِرَةٌ
	Translation			

Review: Lessons 1-3

Question 1: Fill out the following charts using the root of the verb غَفَرَ:

باب التَّفْعِيْل			
الاسم الفاعل	المصدر	المضارع المعروف	الماضي المعروف
الاسم المفعول	المصدر	المضارع المجهول	الماضي المجهول
		النهي	الأمر

باب الْمُفَاعَلَة			
الاسم الفاعل	المصدر	المضارع المعروف	الماضي المعروف
الاسم المفعول	المصدر	المضارع المجهول	الماضي المجهول
		النهي	الأمر

باب الْإِفْعَال			
الاسم الفاعل	المصدر	المضارع المعروف	الماضي المعروف
الاسم المفعول	المصدر	المضارع المجهول	الماضي المجهول
		النهي	الأمر

Question 2: Fill out the following charts using the root of the verb سَكَنَ:

			باب التَّفْعِيْل
الاسم الفاعل	المصدر	المضارع المعروف	الماضي المعروف
الاسم المفعول	المصدر	المضارع المجهول	الماضي المجهول
		النهي	الأمر

			باب الْمُفَاعَلَة
الاسم الفاعل	المصدر	المضارع المعروف	الماضي المعروف
الاسم المفعول	المصدر	المضارع المجهول	الماضي المجهول
		النهي	الأمر

			باب الْإِفْعَال
الاسم الفاعل	المصدر	المضارع المعروف	الماضي المعروف
الاسم المفعول	المصدر	المضارع المجهول	الماضي المجهول
		النهي	الأمر

Question 3: Please fill in the following using the root of the verb كَرُمَ :

al-Tafʿīl al-Fiʿl al-Māḍī al-Muthbat al-Maʿrūf باب التَّفْعِيل-		
	Singular, male, third person	
	Dual, male, third person	
	Plural, male, third person	
	Singular, female, third person	
	Dual, female, third person	
	Plural, female, third person	
	Singular, male, second person	
	Dual, male, second person	
	Plural, male, second person	
	Singular, female, second person	
	Dual, female, second person	
	Plural, female second person	
	Singular, first person	
	Plural, first person	

باب المُفاعَلَة - al-Mufāʿala al-Fiʿl al-Māḍī al-Muthbat al-Majhūl		
	Singular, male, third person	
	Dual, male, third person	
	Plural, male, third person	
	Singular, female, third person	
	Dual, female, third person	
	Plural, female, third person	
	Singular, male, second person	
	Dual, male, second person	
	Plural, male, second person	
	Singular, female, second person	
	Dual, female, second person	
	Plural, female second person	
	Singular, first person	
	Plural, first person	

al-Ifʿāl al-Fiʿl al-Muḍāriʿ al-Muthbat al-Maʿrūf باب الإفْعَال		
	Singular, male, third person	
	Dual, male, third person	
	Plural, male, third person	
	Singular, female, third person	
	Dual, female, third person	
	Plural, female, third person	
	Singular, male, second person	
	Dual, male, second person	
	Plural, male, second person	
	Singular, female, second person	
	Dual, female, second person	
	Plural, female second person	
	Singular, first person	
	Plural, first person	

باب التَّفْعِيل - al-Tafʿīl al-Fiʿl al-Muḍāriʿ al-Manfī al-Majhūl		
	Singular, male, third person	
	Dual, male, third person	
	Plural, male, third person	
	Singular, female, third person	
	Dual, female, third person	
	Plural, female, third person	
	Singular, male, second person	
	Dual, male, second person	
	Plural, male, second person	
	Singular, female, second person	
	Dual, female, second person	
	Plural, female second person	
	Singular, first person	
	Plural, first person	

	al-Mufāʿala al-Fiʿl al-Amr al-Maʿrūf - باب المُفَاعَلَة	
	Singular, male, third person	
	Dual, male, third person	
	Plural, male, third person	
	Singular, female, third person	
	Dual, female, third person	
	Plural, female, third person	
	Singular, male, second person	
	Dual, male, second person	
	Plural, male, second person	
	Singular, female, second person	
	Dual, female, second person	
	Plural, female second person	
	Singular, first person	
	Plural, first person	

Question 4: Translate the following into English:

وَإِنْ كُنْتُمْ مَرْضَى أَوْ عَلَى سَفَرٍ أَوْ جَاءَ أَحَدٌ مِنْكُمْ مِنَ الْغَائِطِ أَوْ لَامَسْتُمُ النِّسَاءَ	(1
إِنَّ اللهَ لَا يُخْلِفُ الْمِيعَادَ	(2
إِنَّهُمْ كَانُوا قَبْلَ ذَٰلِكَ مُتْرَفِينَ	(3
لَا تَبْدِيلَ لِكَلِمَاتِ اللهِ	(4
يَا أَيُّهَا الَّذِينَ آمَنُوا اصْبِرُوا وَصَابِرُوا وَرَابِطُوا	(5

6)	كَلَّمَ اللهُ مُوسٰى تَكْلِيمًا
7)	يُبْطِلُ اللهُ الْبَاطِلَ وَلَوْ كَرِهَ الْمُجْرِمُونَ
8)	وَتَرَكَهُمْ فِي ظُلُمَاتٍ لَا يُبْصِرُونَ
9)	وَأَمَّا بِنِعْمَةِ رَبِّكَ فَحَدِّثْ
10)	كَفِّرْ عَنَّا سَيِّئَاتِنَا

رَبَّنَا إِنَّنَا سَمِعْنَا مُنَادِيًا يُنَادِي لِلْإِيمَانِ أَنْ آمِنُوا بِرَبِّكُمْ فَآمَنَّا	(11
نَحْنُ خَلَقْنَاكُمْ فَلَوْلَا تُصَدِّقُونَ	(12
أَبْشِرُوا بِالْجَنَّةِ الَّتِي كُنْتُمْ تُوعَدُونَ	(13
إِنَّ أَوَّلَ بَيْتٍ وُضِعَ لِلنَّاسِ لَلَّذِي بِبَكَّةَ مُبَارَكًا وَهُدًى لِلْعَالَمِينَ	(14
وَهُمْ عَلَى صَلَاتِهِمْ يُحَافِظُونَ	(15

Question 5: Fill out the following chart:

	Masdar	Verb Form		Arabic
1.	تعليم	Māḍī Manfī Majhūl	Dual, male, second person	
	Translation			
2.	إغلاق	Muḍāriʿ Muthbat Maʿrūf	Plural, first person	
	Translation			
3.	إسراع	Amr Maʿrūf	Singular, male, second person	
	Translation			
4.	معانقة	Nahī Majhūl	Dual, female, third person	
	Translation			
5.	إفهام	Ism Fāʿil	Dual, male	
	Translation			

	Masdar	Verb Form		Arabic
6.	تفريغ	Amr Majhūl	Singular, female, third person	
	Translation			
7.	إسلام	Nahī Majhūl	Dual, male, third person	
	Translation			
8.	مخالفة	Ism Mafʿūl	Singular, female	
	Translation			
9.	تنزيل	Amr Majhūl	Singular, female, second person	
	Translation			
10.	مسارعة	Muḍāriʿ Manfī Maʿrūf	Plural, male, third person	
	Translation			

	Masdar	Verb Form		Arabic
11.				مُنْعَمَتَانِ
	Translation			
12.				لَا نُفَارَقُ
	Translation			
13.				شَاغَلْتُ
	Translation			
14.				لِأُكْرِمْ
	Translation			
15.				مُفْطِرُونَ
	Translation			

Unit 5: The Fifth Pattern – التفعل

This pattern is identified by the number V in the Hans Wehr dictionary.

مُتَفَعِّلٌ	تَفَعُّلًا	يَتَفَعَّلُ	تَفَعَّلَ
الاسم الفاعل	المصدر	المضارع المعروف	الماضي المعروف
مُتَفَعَّلٌ	تَفَعُّلًا	يُتَفَعَّلُ	تُفُعِّلَ
الاسم المفعول	المصدر	المضارع المجهول	الماضي المجهول
		لَا تَفَعَّلْ [2]	تَفَعَّلْ
		النهي	الأمر

---

[2] Whenever there are two تs assembled in the beginning of the pattern of تفعل and تفاعل, one of those تs can be dropped: تتفعل ← تفعل.

Exercises

Question 1: Please fill in the following:

a)

			تَقَبَّلَ
الاسم الفاعل	المصدر	المضارع المعروف	الماضي المعروف
الاسم المفعول	المصدر	المضارع المجهول	الماضي المجهول
		النهي	الأمر

b)

			تَبَسَّمَ
الاسم الفاعل	المصدر	المضارع المعروف	الماضي المعروف
الاسم المفعول	المصدر	المضارع المجهول	الماضي المجهول
		النهي	الأمر

c)

			تَفَكَّهَ
الاسم الفاعل	المصدر	المضارع المعروف	الماضي المعروف
الاسم المفعول	المصدر	المضارع المجهول	الماضي المجهول
		النهي	الأمر

d)

			تَلَبَّثَ
الاسم الفاعل	المصدر	المضارع المعروف	الماضي المعروف
الاسم المفعول	المصدر	المضارع المجهول	الماضي المجهول
		النهي	الأمر

e)

			تَعَجَّلَ
الاسم الفاعل	المصدر	المضارع المعروف	الماضي المعروف
الاسم المفعول	المصدر	المضارع المجهول	الماضي المجهول
		النهي	الأمر

f)

			تَنَفَّرَ
الاسم الفاعل	المصدر	المضارع المعروف	الماضي المعروف
الاسم المفعول	المصدر	المضارع المجهول	الماضي المجهول
		النهي	الأمر

Question 2: Please fill in the following:

al-Tafaʿul al-Fiʿl al-Māḍī al-Muthbat al-Maʿrūf		
	Singular, male, third person	تَجَمَّلَ
	Dual, male, third person	
	Plural, male, third person	
	Singular, female, third person	
	Dual, female, third person	
	Plural, female, third person	
	Singular, male, second person	
	Dual, male, second person	
	Plural, male, second person	
	Singular, female, second person	
	Dual, female, second person	
	Plural, female second person	
	Singular, first person	
	Plural, first person	

al-Tafaʿul al-Fiʿl al-Muḍāriʿ al-Muthbat al-Maʿrūf		
	Singular, male, third person	يَتَفَكَّهُ
	Dual, male, third person	
	Plural, male, third person	
	Singular, female, third person	
	Dual, female, third person	
	Plural, female, third person	
	Singular, male, second person	
	Dual, male, second person	
	Plural, male, second person	
	Singular, female, second person	
	Dual, female, second person	
	Plural, female second person	
	Singular, first person	
	Plural, first person	

al-Tafaʿul al-Fiʿl al-Muḍāriʿ al-Manfī al-Majhūl		
	Singular, male, third person	لَا يُتَقَبَّلُ
	Dual, male, third person	
	Plural, male, third person	
	Singular, female, third person	
	Dual, female, third person	
	Plural, female, third person	
	Singular, male, second person	
	Dual, male, second person	
	Plural, male, second person	
	Singular, female, second person	
	Dual, female, second person	
	Plural, female second person	
	Singular, first person	
	Plural, first person	

al-Tafaʿul al-Fiʿl al-Muḍāriʿ al-Manfī al-Majhūl

al-Tafaʿul al-Fiʿl al-Nahī al-Maʿrūf		
	Singular, male, third person	لَا يَتَبَسَّمْ
	Dual, male, third person	
	Plural, male, third person	
	Singular, female, third person	
	Dual, female, third person	
	Plural, female, third person	
	Singular, male, second person	
	Dual, male, second person	
	Plural, male, second person	
	Singular, female, second person	
	Dual, female, second person	
	Plural, female second person	
	Singular, first person	
	Plural, first person	

Question 3: Translate the following into English:

وَفَاكِهَةٌ مِمَّا يَتَخَيَّرُونَ	(1
تَمَيَّزُ الْجَهَنَّمُ مِنَ الْغَيْظِ	(2
تَنَزَّلُ الْمَلَائِكَةُ وَالرُّوحُ فِي لَيْلَةِ الْقَدْرِ بِإِذْنِ رَبِّهِم	(3
أَفَلَا يَتَدَبَّرُونَ الْقُرْآنَ	(4
فَتَرَبَّصُوا إِنَّا مَعَكُم مُّتَرَبِّصُونَ	(5

جَعَلْنَا حَرَمًا آمِنًا وَيُتَخَطَّفُ النَّاسُ مِنْ حَوْلِهِمْ _____ _____	(6
خَرَجَ مُوسَى مِنْهَا خَائِفًا يَتَرَقَّبُ _____ _____	(7
فَأَخَذْنَاهُم بِالْبَأْسَاءِ وَالضَّرَّاءِ لَعَلَّهُمْ يَتَضَرَّعُونَ _____ _____	(8
مَا هَذَا إِلَّا بَشَرٌ مِّثْلُكُمْ يُرِيدُ أَن يَتَفَضَّلَ عَلَيْكُمْ _____ _____	(9
يَتَفَيَّأُ ظِلَالُ خَلْقِ اللهِ عَنِ الْيَمِينِ وَالشَّمَائِلِ سُجَّدًا لِلّهِ _____ _____	(10

فَيَتَعَلَّمُونَ مِنْهُمَا مَا يُفَرِّقُونَ بِهِ بَيْنَ الْمَرْءِ وَزَوْجِهِ	11)
أَوَلَمْ يَرَوْا إِلَى مَا خَلَقَ اللهُ مِن شَيْءٍ يَتَفَيَّأُ ظِلَالُهُ عَنِ الْيَمِينِ وَالشَّمَائِلِ سُجَّدًا لِلّهِ وَهُمْ دَاخِرُونَ	12)
لَا يَتَكَلَّمُونَ إِلَّا مَنْ أَذِنَ لَهُ الرَّحْمَنُ وَقَالَ صَوَابًا	13)
ذَرْهُمْ يَأْكُلُوا وَيَتَمَتَّعُوا	14)
يَا أَيُّهَا الَّذِينَ آمَنُوا إِن جَاءَكُمْ فَاسِقٌ بِنَبَإٍ فَتَبَيَّنُوا	15)

Question 4: Fill out the following chart:

	Masdar	Verb Form		Arabic
1.	تفكر	Ism Fāʿil	Dual, female	
	Translation			
2.	تحدث	Muḍāriʿ Muthbat Maʿrūf	Plural, female, third person	
	Translation			
3.	تحرر	Māḍī Manfī Maʿrūf	Dual, male, second person	
	Translation			
4.	تعرف	Ism Mafʿūl	Singular, female	
	Translation			
5.	تحسن	Amr Maʿrūf	Plural, male, third person	
	Translation			

	Masdar	Verb Form		Arabic
6.	تعجب	Nahī Maʿrūf	Dual, female, third person	
	Translation			
7.	تشرف	Muḍāriʿ Manfī Majhūl	Plural, first person	
	Translation			
8.	تصدق	Ism Mafʿūl	Singular, male	
	Translation			
9.	تدين	Muḍāriʿ Manfī Maʿrūf	First person, singular	
	Translation			
10.	تضرع	Māḍī Muthbat Maʿrūf	Plural, male, third person	
	Translation			

Masdar	Verb Form		Arabic
11.			لِتَتَغَلَّبُوا
Translation			
12.			مُتَكَلِّمَانِ
Translation			
13.			مَا تُحُرِّكَ
Translation			
14.			لَا تَتَعَلَّمْنَ
Translation			
15.			مُتَحَسِّرَتَانِ
Translation			

Unit 6: The Sixth Pattern – التفاعل

This pattern is identified by the number VI in the Hans Wehr dictionary. This pattern is often used to refer to an action which is performed mutually.

مُتَفَاعِلٌ	تَفَاعُلًا	يَتَفَاعَلُ	تَفَاعَلَ
الاسم الفاعل	المصدر	المضارع المعروف	الماضي المعروف
مُتَفَاعَلٌ	تَفَاعُلًا	يُتَفَاعَلُ	تُفُوعِلَ
الاسم المفعول	المصدر	المضارع المجهول	الماضي المجهول
	لَا تَفَاعَلْ ³		تَفَاعَلْ
	النهي		الأمر

---

³ Whenever there are two تs assembled in the beginning of the pattern of تفعل and تفاعل, one of those تs can be dropped: تتفعل ← تفعل.

Exercises

Question 1: Please fill in the following:

a)

			تَقَابَلَ
الاسم الفاعل	المصدر	المضارع المعروف	الماضي المعروف
الاسم المفعول	المصدر	المضارع المجهول	الماضي المجهول
		النهي	الأمر

b)

			تَفَاخَرَ
الاسم الفاعل	المصدر	المضارع المعروف	الماضي المعروف
الاسم المفعول	المصدر	المضارع المجهول	الماضي المجهول
		النهي	الأمر

c)

			تَعَارَفَ
الاسم الفاعل	المصدر	المضارع المعروف	الماضي المعروف
الاسم المفعول	المصدر	المضارع المجهول	الماضي المجهول
		النهي	الأمر

d)

الاسم الفاعل	المصدر	المضارع المعروف	تَنَاقَصَ
			الماضي المعروف
الاسم المفعول	المصدر	المضارع المجهول	الماضي المجهول
		النهي	الأمر

e)

الاسم الفاعل	المصدر	المضارع المعروف	تَقَاتَلَ
			الماضي المعروف
الاسم المفعول	المصدر	المضارع المجهول	الماضي المجهول
		النهي	الأمر

f)

الاسم الفاعل	المصدر	المضارع المعروف	تَصَاعَبَ
			الماضي المعروف
الاسم المفعول	المصدر	المضارع المجهول	الماضي المجهول
		النهي	الأمر

Question 2: Please fill in the following:

al-Tafāʿul al-Fiʿl al-Māḍī al-Manfī al-Maʿrūf		
	Singular, male, third person	ما تَنَاسَبَ
	Dual, male, third person	
	Plural, male, third person	
	Singular, female, third person	
	Dual, female, third person	
	Plural, female, third person	
	Singular, male, second person	
	Dual, male, second person	
	Plural, male, second person	
	Singular, female, second person	
	Dual, female, second person	
	Plural, female second person	
	Singular, first person	
	Plural, first person	

al-Tafāʿul al-Fiʿl al-Muḍāriʿ al-Muthbat al-Maʿrūf		
	Singular, male, third person	يَتَنَاوَلُ
	Dual, male, third person	
	Plural, male, third person	
	Singular, female, third person	
	Dual, female, third person	
	Plural, female, third person	
	Singular, male, second person	
	Dual, male, second person	
	Plural, male, second person	
	Singular, female, second person	
	Dual, female, second person	
	Plural, female second person	
	Singular, first person	
	Plural, first person	

al-Tafāʿul al-Fiʿl al-Muḍāriʿ al-Manfī al-Majhūl		
	Singular, male, third person	لَا يُتَنَاقَصُ
	Dual, male, third person	
	Plural, male, third person	
	Singular, female, third person	
	Dual, female, third person	
	Plural, female, third person	
	Singular, male, second person	
	Dual, male, second person	
	Plural, male, second person	
	Singular, female, second person	
	Dual, female, second person	
	Plural, female second person	
	Singular, first person	
	Plural, first person	

al-Tafāʿul al-Fiʿl al-Amr al-Maʿrūf		
	Singular, male, third person	لِيَتَعَارَف
	Dual, male, third person	
	Plural, male, third person	
	Singular, female, third person	
	Dual, female, third person	
	Plural, female, third person	
	Singular, male, second person	
	Dual, male, second person	
	Plural, male, second person	
	Singular, female, second person	
	Dual, female, second person	
	Plural, female second person	
	Singular, first person	
	Plural, first person	

Question 3: Translate the following into English:

مِنْهُ آيَاتٌ مُحْكَمَاتٌ هُنَّ أُمُّ الْكِتَابِ وَأُخَرُ مُتَشَابِهَاتٌ _____ _____	(1
وَلَا تَلْمِزُوا أَنْفُسَكُمْ وَلَا تَنَابَزُوا بِالْأَلْقَابِ _____ _____	(2
إِذْ يَتَنَازَعُونَ بَيْنَهُمْ _____	(3
كَذَلِكَ بَعَثْنَاهُمْ لِيَتَسَاءَلُوا بَيْنَهُمْ _____	(4
يَتَدَارَكَنِي اللهُ بِرَحْمَةٍ _____	(5

6)	وَفِي ذٰلِكَ فَلْيَتَنَافَسِ الْمُتَنَافِسُونَ
7)	دَخَلْتُ عَلَى عُبَادَةَ، وَهُوَ مَرِيضٌ أَتَخَايَلُ فِيهِ الْمَوْتَ
8)	يُرِيدُونَ أَنْ يَتَحَاكَمُوا إِلَى الطَّاغُوتِ وَقَدْ أُمِرُوا أَنْ يَكْفُرُوا بِهِ
9)	فَإِنْ طَلَّقَهَا فَلَا جُنَاحَ عَلَيْهِمَا أَنْ يَتَرَاجَعَا إِنْ ظَنَّا أَنْ يُقِيمَا حُدُودَ اللهِ
10)	إِنَّ أَهْلَ الْجَنَّةِ يَتَرَاءَوْنَ أَهْلَ الْغُرَفِ مِنْ فَوْقِهِمْ

لَوْلَا أَن تَدَارَكَهُ نِعْمَةٌ مِّن رَّبِّهِ لَنُبِذَ بِالْعَرَاءِ وَهُوَ مَذْمُومٌ _____ _____	(11
ثُمَّ أَنتُمْ هَٰؤُلَاءِ تَقْتُلُونَ أَنفُسَكُمْ وَتُخْرِجُونَ فَرِيقًا مِّنكُم مِّن دِيَارِهِمْ تَظَاهَرُونَ عَلَيْهِم بِالْإِثْمِ وَالْعُدْوَانِ _____ _____ _____	(12
وَيَوْمَ يَحْشُرُهُمْ كَأَن لَّمْ يَلْبَثُوا إِلَّا سَاعَةً مِّنَ النَّهَارِ يَتَعَارَفُونَ بَيْنَهُمْ _____ _____	(13
يَوْمَ يَجْمَعُكُمْ لِيَوْمِ الْجَمْعِ ذَٰلِكَ يَوْمُ التَّغَابُنِ _____ _____	(14
فِي جَنَّاتِ النَّعِيمِ - عَلَىٰ سُرُرٍ مُّتَقَابِلِينَ _____ _____	(15

Question 4: Fill out the following chart:

	Masdar	Verb Form		Arabic
1.	تناصر	Amr Majhūl	Plural, female, second person	
	Translation			
2.	تبادل	Nahī Maʿrūf	Singular, male, third person	
	Translation			
3.	تباعد	Muḍāriʿ Manfī Maʿrūf	Dual, male, second person	
	Translation			
4.	تداخل	Ism Mafʿūl	Dual, male	
	Translation			
5.	تنازع	Muḍāriʿ Manfī Majhūl	Plural, first person	
	Translation			

	Masdar	Verb Form		Arabic
6.	تحاسد	Māḍī Muthbat Maʿrūf	Singular, male, second person.	
	Translation			
7.	تذاكر	Amr Maʿrūf	Singular, first person	
	Translation			
8.	تحامل	Ism Mafʿūl	Plural, male	
	Translation			
9.	تصالح	Ism Fāʿil	Plural, female	
	Translation			
10.	تضاحك	Amr Maʿrūf	Dual, male, second person	
	Translation			

	Masdar		Verb Form	Arabic
11.				لَا يَتَفَاهَمْ
	Translation			
12.				لَا تُتَقَابَلُونَ
	Translation			
13.				تُكُوتِينَ
	Translation			
14.				مُتَمَاثَلَتَانِ
	Translation			
15.				مُتَمَاسِكَاتٌ
	Translation			

Unit 7: The Seventh Pattern – الانفعال

مُنْفَعِلٌ	اِنْفِعَالًا	يَنْفَعِلُ	اِنْفَعَلَ
الاسم الفاعل	المصدر	المضارع المعروف	الماضي المعروف
-	-	-	-
الاسم المفعول	المصدر	المضارع المجهول	الماضي المجهول
		لَا تَنْفَعِلْ	اِنْفَعِلْ
		النهي	الأمر

Exercises

Question 1: Please fill in the following:

a)

			انْفَطَرَ
الاسم الفاعل	المصدر	المضارع المعروف	الماضي المعروف
الاسم المفعول	المصدر	المضارع المجهول	الماضي المجهول
		النهي	الأمر

b)

			انْقَلَبَ
الاسم الفاعل	المصدر	المضارع المعروف	الماضي المعروف
الاسم المفعول	المصدر	المضارع المجهول	الماضي المجهول
		النهي	الأمر

c)

			انْصَرَفَ
الاسم الفاعل	المصدر	المضارع المعروف	الماضي المعروف
الاسم المفعول	المصدر	المضارع المجهول	الماضي المجهول
		النهي	الأمر

d)

			اِنْشَعَبَ
الاسم الفاعل	المصدر	المضارع المعروف	الماضي المعروف
الاسم المفعول	المصدر	المضارع المجهول	الماضي المجهول
		النهي	الأمر

e)

			اِنْكَسَرَ
الاسم الفاعل	المصدر	المضارع المعروف	الماضي المعروف
الاسم المفعول	المصدر	المضارع المجهول	الماضي المجهول
		النهي	الأمر

f)

			اِنْخَدَعَ
الاسم الفاعل	المصدر	المضارع المعروف	الماضي المعروف
الاسم المفعول	المصدر	المضارع المجهول	الماضي المجهول
		النهي	الأمر

Question 2: Please fill in the following:

al-Infiʿāl al-Fiʿl al-Mādī al-Muthbat al-Maʿrūf		
	Singular, male, third person	انْقَلَبَ
	Dual, male, third person	
	Plural, male, third person	
	Singular, female, third person	
	Dual, female, third person	
	Plural, female, third person	
	Singular, male, second person	
	Dual, male, second person	
	Plural, male, second person	
	Singular, female, second person	
	Dual, female, second person	
	Plural, female second person	
	Singular, first person	
	Plural, first person	

al-Infiʿāl al-Fiʿl al-Muḍāriʿ al-Muthbat al-Maʿrūf		
	Singular, male, third person	يَنْگَسِرُ
	Dual, male, third person	
	Plural, male, third person	
	Singular, female, third person	
	Dual, female, third person	
	Plural, female, third person	
	Singular, male, second person	
	Dual, male, second person	
	Plural, male, second person	
	Singular, female, second person	
	Dual, female, second person	
	Plural, female second person	
	Singular, first person	
	Plural, first person	

al-Infiʿāl al-Fiʿl al-Muḍāriʿ al-Manfī al-Maʿrūf

	Singular, male, third person	لَا يَنْفَطِرُ
	Dual, male, third person	
	Plural, male, third person	
	Singular, female, third person	
	Dual, female, third person	
	Plural, female, third person	
	Singular, male, second person	
	Dual, male, second person	
	Plural, male, second person	
	Singular, female, second person	
	Dual, female, second person	
	Plural, female second person	
	Singular, first person	
	Plural, first person	

		al-Infiʿāl al-Fiʿl al-Nahī al-Maʿrūf
	Singular, male, third person	لَا يَنْصَرِفْ
	Dual, male, third person	
	Plural, male, third person	
	Singular, female, third person	
	Dual, female, third person	
	Plural, female, third person	
	Singular, male, second person	
	Dual, male, second person	
	Plural, male, second person	
	Singular, female, second person	
	Dual, female, second person	
	Plural, female second person	
	Singular, first person	
	Plural, first person	

al-Infiʿāl al-Fiʿl al-Nahī al-Maʿrūf

Question 3: Translate the following into English:

1)	يَنْقَلِبْ إِلَيْكَ الْبَصَرُ خَاسِئًا
2)	كَرِهَ اللهُ انْبِعَاثَهُمْ فَثَبَّطَهُمْ
3)	انْطَلِقُوا إِلَى ظِلٍّ ذِي ثَلَاثِ شُعَبٍ
4)	عَنْ أَبِي هُرَيْرَةَ، أَنَّ النَّبِيَّ صَلَّى اللهُ عَلَيْهِ وَسَلَّمَ لَقِيَهُ وَهُوَ جُنُبٌ، قَالَ: فَانْبَجَسْتُ
5)	فَخَرَجَ مُنْطَلِقًا نَحْوَ حُجْرَةِ عَائِشَةَ

فَغُلِبُوا هُنَالِكَ وَانْقَلَبُوا صَاغِرِينَ	(6
وَلَّيْتُ مُنْصَرِفًا	(7
فَانْطَلَقَا حَتَّى إِذَا لَقِيَا غُلَامًا	(8
انْبَعَثَ رَجُلٌ عَزِيزٌ عَارِمٌ	(9
إِنَّ جِبْرِيلَ عَلَيْهِ السَّلَامُ كَانَ يَلْقَا رَسُولَ اللهِ، فِي كُلِّ سَنَةٍ، فِي رَمَضَانَ حَتَّى يَنْسَلِخَ	(10

(11)	سَقَطَتِ الصَّحْفَةُ فَانْفَلَقَتْ
(12)	انْطَلَقَا حَتّى إِذَا رَكِبَا فِي السَّفِينَةِ
(13)	لَا انْفِصَامَ لِلْعُرْوَةِ الْوُثْقَى
(14)	انْقَلَبُوا بِنِعْمَةٍ مِنَ اللهِ وَفَضْلٍ
(15)	إِذَا السَّمَاءُ انْفَطَرَتْ

Question 4: Fill out the following chart:

	Masdar	Verb Form		Arabic
1.	انطلاق	Ism Fāʿil	Plural, male	
	Translation			
2.	انبساط	Ism Fāʿil	Plural, female	
	Translation			
3.	انخفاض	Amr Maʿrūf	Dual, male, second person	
	Translation			
4.	انشراح	Nahī Maʿrūf	Plural, male, third person	
	Translation			
5.	انحراف	Muḍāriʿ Manfī Maʿrūf	Plural, male, second person	
	Translation			

	Masdar	Verb Form		Arabic
6.	انعطاف	Māḍī Muthbat Maʿrūf	Plural, female, third person	
	Translation			
7.	انخراق	Ism Fāʿil	Dual, female	
	Translation			
8.	اندفاع	Ism Fāʿil	Plural, female	
	Translation			
9.	انصراف	Muḍāriʿ Manfī Maʿrūf	Singular, first person	
	Translation			
10.	انقلاب	Amr, Maʿrūf	Plural, first person	
	Translation			

Masdar	Verb Form		Arabic
11.			لَا تَنْفَصِلْ
Translation			
12.			مُنْفَلِقُونَ
Translation			
13.			مَا انْكَسَرْتِ
Translation			
14.			يَنْعَصِرُ
Translation			
15.			مُنْغَمِسَاتٌ
Translation			

Review: Lessons 1-6

Question 1: Fill out the following charts using the root of the verb كَسَرَ[4]:

باب التَّفْعِيْل			
الاسم الفاعل	المصدر	المضارع المعروف	الماضي المعروف
الاسم المفعول	المصدر	المضارع المجهول	الماضي المجهول
		النهي	الأمر

باب الْمُفَاعَلَة			
الاسم الفاعل	المصدر	المضارع المعروف	الماضي المعروف
الاسم المفعول	المصدر	المضارع المجهول	الماضي المجهول
		النهي	الأمر

باب الْإِفْعَال			
الاسم الفاعل	المصدر	المضارع المعروف	الماضي المعروف
الاسم المفعول	المصدر	المضارع المجهول	الماضي المجهول
		النهي	الأمر

---

[4] Some of these are purely for the sake of practicing morphology, and they may not be actual verbs.

باب التَّفَعُّل			
الاسم الفاعل	المصدر	المضارع المعروف	الماضي المعروف
الاسم المفعول	المصدر	المضارع المجهول	الماضي المجهول
		النهي	الأمر

باب التَّفَاعُل			
الاسم الفاعل	المصدر	المضارع المعروف	الماضي المعروف
الاسم المفعول	المصدر	المضارع المجهول	الماضي المجهول
		النهي	الأمر

باب الْاِنْفِعَال			
الاسم الفاعل	المصدر	المضارع المعروف	الماضي المعروف
الاسم المفعول	المصدر	المضارع المجهول	الماضي المجهول
		النهي	الأمر

Question 2: Fill in the following using the root of the verb written in brackets:

باب التَّفَعُّل – al-Tafaʿul al-Fiʿl al-Māḍī al-Muthbat al-Maʿrūf (ذكر)	
	Singular, male, third person	
	Dual, male, third person	
	Plural, male, third person	
	Singular, female, third person	
	Dual, female, third person	
	Plural, female, third person	
	Singular, male, second person	
	Dual, male, second person	
	Plural, male, second person	
	Singular, female, second person	
	Dual, female, second person	
	Plural, female second person	
	Singular, first person	
	Plural, first person	

al-Tafāʿul al-Fiʿl al-Māḍī al-Muthbat al-Majhūl (كتب) باب التَّفَاعُل-		
	Singular, male, third person	
	Dual, male, third person	
	Plural, male, third person	
	Singular, female, third person	
	Dual, female, third person	
	Plural, female, third person	
	Singular, male, second person	
	Dual, male, second person	
	Plural, male, second person	
	Singular, female, second person	
	Dual, female, second person	
	Plural, female second person	
	Singular, first person	
	Plural, first person	

al-Infiʿāl al-Fiʿl al-Muḍāriʿ al-Muthbat al-Maʿrūf (فصل) - باب الْإِنْفِعَال		
	Singular, male, third person	
	Dual, male, third person	
	Plural, male, third person	
	Singular, female, third person	
	Dual, female, third person	
	Plural, female, third person	
	Singular, male, second person	
	Dual, male, second person	
	Plural, male, second person	
	Singular, female, second person	
	Dual, female, second person	
	Plural, female second person	
	Singular, first person	
	Plural, first person	

al-Tafʿīl al-Fiʿl al-Muḍāriʿ al-Manfī al-Majhūl (حمد) - باب التَّفْعِيل		
	Singular, male, third person	
	Dual, male, third person	
	Plural, male, third person	
	Singular, female, third person	
	Dual, female, third person	
	Plural, female, third person	
	Singular, male, second person	
	Dual, male, second person	
	Plural, male, second person	
	Singular, female, second person	
	Dual, female, second person	
	Plural, female second person	
	Singular, first person	
	Plural, first person	

	(عرض) al-Mufāʿala al-Fiʿl al-Amr al-Maʿrūf - باب المُفَاعَلَة	
	Singular, male, third person	
	Dual, male, third person	
	Plural, male, third person	
	Singular, female, third person	
	Dual, female, third person	
	Plural, female, third person	
	Singular, male, second person	
	Dual, male, second person	
	Plural, male, second person	
	Singular, female, second person	
	Dual, female, second person	
	Plural, female second person	
	Singular, first person	
	Plural, first person	

al-Ifʿāl al-Fiʿl al–Nahī al-Maʿrūf (قبل) - باب الْإِفْعَالْ		
	Singular, male, third person	
	Dual, male, third person	
	Plural, male, third person	
	Singular, female, third person	
	Dual, female, third person	
	Plural, female, third person	
	Singular, male, second person	
	Dual, male, second person	
	Plural, male, second person	
	Singular, female, second person	
	Dual, female, second person	
	Plural, female second person	
	Singular, first person	
	Plural, first person	

Question 3: Translate the following into English:

1)	نَزَلَ اللهُ إِلَى السَّمَاءِ الدُّنْيَا، فَيَقُولُ: هَلْ مِنْ تَائِبٍ؟ هَلْ مِنْ سَائِلٍ؟ هَلْ مِنْ دَاعٍ؟ حَتَّى يَنْفَجِرَ الْفَجْرُ
	_____
	_____
	_____
2)	إِنَّا إِلَى رَبِّنَا مُنْقَلِبُونَ
	_____
3)	وَإِنْ كُنْتُمْ مَرْضَى أَوْ عَلَى سَفَرٍ أَوْ جَاءَ أَحَدٌ مِنْكُمْ مِنَ الْغَائِطِ أَوْ لَامَسْتُمُ النِّسَاءَ فَلَمْ تَجِدُوا مَاءً فَتَيَمَّمُوا صَعِيدًا طَيِّبًا
	_____
	_____
	_____
4)	اضْرِبْ بِعَصَاكَ الْحَجَرَ فَانْفَجَرَتْ مِنْهُ اثْنَتَا عَشْرَةَ عَيْنًا
	_____
	_____
	_____
5)	وَمَا يَعْلَمُ تَأْوِيلَهُ إِلَّا اللهُ
	_____

6)	وَيَتَفَكَّرُونَ فِي خَلْقِ السَّمَاوَاتِ وَالْأَرْضِ رَبَّنَا مَا خَلَقْتَ هَٰذَا بَاطِلًا
7)	وَبَشِّرِ الَّذِينَ آمَنُوا وَعَمِلُوا الصَّالِحَاتِ أَنَّ لَهُمْ جَنَّاتٍ تَجْرِي مِنْ تَحْتِهَا الْأَنْهَارُ كُلَّمَا رُزِقُوا مِنْهَا مِنْ ثَمَرَةٍ رِزْقًا قَالُوا هَٰذَا الَّذِي رُزِقْنَا مِنْ قَبْلُ وَأُتُوا بِهِ مُتَشَابِهًا
8)	هَٰذَا يَوْمُكُمُ الَّذِي كُنْتُمْ تُوعَدُونَ
9)	وَإِذَا مَرُّوا بِهِمْ يَتَغَامَزُونَ
10)	وَإِذَا النُّجُومُ انْكَدَرَتْ

11)	فَإِنْ تَنَازَعْتُمْ فِي شَيْءٍ فَرُدُّوهُ إِلَى اللهِ وَالرَّسُولِ
12)	يَا أَيُّهَا الَّذِينَ آمَنُوا لَا تَأْكُلُوا الرِّبَا أَضْعَافًا مُضَاعَفَةً
13)	حُرِّمَتْ عَلَيْكُمُ الْمَيْتَةُ وَالدَّمُ وَلَحْمُ الْخِنْزِيرِ وَالْمُنْخَنِقَةُ
14)	رَبَّنَا أَبْصَرْنَا وَسَمِعْنَا فَارْجِعْنَا نَعْمَلْ صَالِحًا
15)	الَّذِينَ يُؤْمِنُونَ بِمَا أُنْزِلَ إِلَيْكَ وَمَا أُنْزِلَ مِنْ قَبْلِكَ

Question 4: Fill out the following chart:

	Masdar	Pattern	Verb Form		Arabic
1.	تحرير		Muḍāriʿ Manfī Majhūl	Singular, first person	
	Translation				
2.	محاسنة		Amr, Maʿrūf	Plural, first person	
	Translation				
3.	تكسير		Nahī Maʿrūf	Singular, male, second person	
	Translation				
4.	تحرر		Ism Fāʿil	Plural, male	
	Translation				
5.	تكائُب		Māḍī Manfī Majhūl	Singular, female, second person	
	Translation				

	Masdar	Pattern	Verb Form		Arabic
6.	تصديق		Muḍāriʿ Muthbat Maʿrūf	Singular, male, third person	
	Translation				
7.	تحسّن		Ism Fāʿil	Plural, female	
	Translation				
8.	انفصال		Amr Maʿrūf	Singular, male, second person	
	Translation				
9.	انكسار		Nahī Maʿrūf	Plural, first person	
	Translation				
10.	تبديل		Muḍāriʿ Manfī Majhūl	Plural, male, third person	
	Translation				

	Masdar	Pattern	Verb Form		Arabic
11.					مَا تُصُولِحْتُ
	Translation				
12.					مُتَحَاشَدَتَانِ
	Translation				
13.					مُتَفَكِّرُونَ
	Translation				
14.					لِتَنْقَلِبَا
	Translation				
15.					لَا يُبَشَّرْ
	Translation				

Unit 8: The Eighth Pattern – الافتعال

This pattern is identified by the number VIII in the Hans Wehr dictionary.

مُفْتَعِلٌ	اِفْتِعَالًا	يَفْتَعِلُ	اِفْتَعَلَ
الاسم الفاعل	المصدر	المضارع المعروف	الماضي المعروف
مُفْتَعَلٌ	اِفْتِعالا	يُفْتَعَلُ	أُفْتُعِلَ
الاسم المفعول	المصدر	المضارع المجهول	الماضي المجهول
		لَا تَفْتَعِلْ	اِفْتَعِلْ
		النهي	الأمر

Exercises

Question 1: Please fill in the following:

a)

			اجْتَنَبَ
الاسم الفاعل	المصدر	المضارع المعروف	الماضي المعروف
الاسم المفعول	المصدر	المضارع المجهول	الماضي المجهول
		النهي	الأمر

b)

			اعْتَزَلَ
الاسم الفاعل	المصدر	المضارع المعروف	الماضي المعروف
الاسم المفعول	المصدر	المضارع المجهول	الماضي المجهول
		النهي	الأمر

c)

			اقْتَنَصَ
الاسم الفاعل	المصدر	المضارع المعروف	الماضي المعروف
الاسم المفعول	المصدر	المضارع المجهول	الماضي المجهول
		النهي	الأمر

d)

			الْتَمَسَ
الاسم الفاعل	المصدر	المضارع المعروف	الماضي المعروف
الاسم المفعول	المصدر	المضارع المجهول	الماضي المجهول
		النهي	الأمر

e)

			اقْتَرَبَ
الاسم الفاعل	المصدر	المضارع المعروف	الماضي المعروف
الاسم المفعول	المصدر	المضارع المجهول	الماضي المجهول
		النهي	الأمر

f)

			اجْتَمَعَ
الاسم الفاعل	المصدر	المضارع المعروف	الماضي المعروف
الاسم المفعول	المصدر	المضارع المجهول	الماضي المجهول
		النهي	الأمر

Question 2: Please fill in the following:

al-Iftiʿāl al-Fiʿl al-Māḍī al-Muthbat al-Maʿrūf		
	Singular, male, third person	اسْتَمَعَ
	Dual, male, third person	
	Plural, male, third person	
	Singular, female, third person	
	Dual, female, third person	
	Plural, female, third person	
	Singular, male, second person	
	Dual, male, second person	
	Plural, male, second person	
	Singular, female, second person	
	Dual, female, second person	
	Plural, female second person	
	Singular, first person	
	Plural, first person	

al-Iftiʿāl al-Fiʿl al-Muḍāriʿ al-Muthbat al-Maʿrūf		
	Singular, male, third person	يَخْتَلِفُ
	Dual, male, third person	
	Plural, male, third person	
	Singular, female, third person	
	Dual, female, third person	
	Plural, female, third person	
	Singular, male, second person	
	Dual, male, second person	
	Plural, male, second person	
	Singular, female, second person	
	Dual, female, second person	
	Plural, female second person	
	Singular, first person	
	Plural, first person	

al-Iftiʿāl al-Fiʿl al-Muḍāriʿ al-Muthbat al-Maʿrūf

al-Iftiʿāl al-Fiʿl al-Muḍāriʿ al-Manfī al-Majhūl

	Singular, male, third person	لَا يُجْتَنَبُ
	Dual, male, third person	
	Plural, male, third person	
	Singular, female, third person	
	Dual, female, third person	
	Plural, female, third person	
	Singular, male, second person	
	Dual, male, second person	
	Plural, male, second person	
	Singular, female, second person	
	Dual, female, second person	
	Plural, female second person	
	Singular, first person	
	Plural, first person	

al-Iftiʿāl al-Fiʿl al-Amr al-Maʿrūf		
	Singular, male, third person	لِيَقْتَرِبْ
	Dual, male, third person	
	Plural, male, third person	
	Singular, female, third person	
	Dual, female, third person	
	Plural, female, third person	
	Singular, male, second person	
	Dual, male, second person	
	Plural, male, second person	
	Singular, female, second person	
	Dual, female, second person	
	Plural, female second person	
	Singular, first person	
	Plural, first person	

Question 3: Translate the following into English:

وَاللهُ عَزِيزٌ ذُو انْتِقَامٍ	(1
وَمَا اخْتَلَفَ الَّذِينَ أُوتُوا الْكِتَابَ إِلَّا مِنْ بَعْدِ مَا جَاءَهُمُ الْعِلْمُ	(2
اعْتَرَفُوا بِذَنْبِهِمْ	(3
أُولَئِكَ الَّذِينَ امْتَحَنَ اللهُ قُلُوبَهُمْ لِلتَّقْوَى	(4
وَإِنْ طَائِفَتَانِ مِنَ الْمُؤْمِنِينَ اقْتَتَلُوا فَأَصْلِحُوا بَيْنَهُمَا	(5

يَا أَيُّهَا الَّذِينَ آمَنُوا اجْتَنِبُوا كَثِيرًا مِنَ الظَّنِّ إِنَّ بَعْضَ الظَّنِّ إِثْمٌ _____ _____	(6
إِنَّ قَوْمًا يُخْرَجُونَ مِنَ النَّارِ يَحْتَرِقُونَ فِيهَا، إِلَّا دَارَاتِ وُجُوهِهِمْ حَتَّى يَدْخُلُونَ الْجَنَّةَ _____ _____	(7
وَمَا كُنْتُمْ تَسْتَتِرُونَ أَنْ يَشْهَدَ عَلَيْكُمْ سَمْعُكُمْ وَلَا أَبْصَارُكُمْ وَلَا جُلُودُكُمْ _____ _____	(8
ارْتَقِبْ يَوْمَ تَأْتِي السَّمَاءُ بِدُخَانٍ مُبِينٍ _____	(9
وَالَّذِينَ يُؤْذُونَ الْمُؤْمِنِينَ وَالْمُؤْمِنَاتِ بِغَيْرِ مَا اكْتَسَبُوا فَقَدِ احْتَمَلُوا بُهْتَانًا وَإِثْمًا مُبِينًا _____ _____	(10

وَاضْرِبْ لَهُمْ مَثَلَ الْحَيَاةِ الدُّنْيَا كَمَاءٍ أَنْزَلْنَاهُ مِنَ السَّمَاءِ فَاخْتَلَطَ بِهِ نَبَاتُ الْأَرْضِ _____ _____ _____	(11
اسْتَمَعَ نَفَرٌ مِنَ الْجِنِّ فَقَالُوا إِنَّا سَمِعْنَا قُرْآنًا عَجَبًا _____ _____ _____	(12
وَحَفِظْنَاهَا مِنْ كُلِّ شَيْطَانٍ رَجِيمٍ إِلَّا مَنِ اسْتَرَقَ السَّمْعَ فَأَتْبَعَهُ شِهَابٌ مُبِينٌ _____ _____ _____	(13
وَلَوْ شَاءَ رَبُّكَ لَجَعَلَ النَّاسَ أُمَّةً وَاحِدَةً وَلَا يَزَالُونَ مُخْتَلِفِينَ _____ _____ _____	(14
وَارْتَقِبُوا إِنِّي مَعَكُمْ رَقِيبٌ _____ _____	(15

Question 4: Fill out the following chart:

Masdar	Verb Form		Arabic
1. ابتداع	Amr Maʿrūf	Plural, first person	
Translation			
2. ابتذال	Māḍī Muthbat Majhūl	Singular, first person	
Translation			
3. ابتراد	Muḍāriʿ Muthbat Maʿrūf	Singular, female, second person	
Translation			
4. ابتسام	Māḍī Manfī Maʿrūf	Plural, male, second person	
Translation			
5. اقتراب	Nahī Maʿrūf	Dual, female, third person	
Translation			

	Masdar	Verb Form		Arabic
6.	ابتهاج	Ism Fāʿil	Plural, female	
	Translation			
7.	احتقار	Amr Majhūl	Singular, male, second person	
	Translation			
8.	احتفاظ	Nahī Maʿrūf	Plural, first person	
	Translation			
9.	اقتراض	Māḍī Manfī Majhūl	Dual, male, second person	
	Translation			
10.	افتراض	Muḍāriʿ Manfī Majhūl	Singular, first person	
	Translation			

	Masdar	Verb Form		Arabic
11.				مُغْتَسَلَانِ
	Translation			
12.				مُغْتَبِطَاتٌ
	Translation			
13.				لِتُفْتَرَقَا
	Translation			
14.				لَا يُلْتَمَسَا
	Translation			
15.				مُشْتَعِلَتَانِ
	Translation			

Unit 9: The Ninth Pattern – الافعلال

This pattern is identified by the number IX in the Hans Wehr dictionary. This pattern is always Lāzim which means that it does not get majhūl verbs, mafʿūl bihīs and ism mafʿūls. This pattern is often used to express colours.

مُفْعَلٌّ	اِفْعِلَالًا	يَفْعَلُّ	اِفْعَلَّ
الاسم الفاعل	المصدر	المضارع المعروف	الماضي المعروف
---	---	---	---
الاسم المفعول	المصدر	المضارع المجهول	الماضي المجهول
		لَا تَفْعَلَّ	اِفْعَلَّ
		النهي	الأمر

Exercises

Question 1: Please fill in the following:

a)

			اِحْمَرَّ
الاسم الفاعل	المصدر	المضارع المعروف	الماضي المعروف
الاسم المفعول	المصدر	المضارع المجهول	الماضي المجهول
		النهي	الأمر

b)

			اِسْوَدَّ
الاسم الفاعل	المصدر	المضارع المعروف	الماضي المعروف
الاسم المفعول	المصدر	المضارع المجهول	الماضي المجهول
		النهي	الأمر

c)

			اِخْضَرَّ
الاسم الفاعل	المصدر	المضارع المعروف	الماضي المعروف
الاسم المفعول	المصدر	المضارع المجهول	الماضي المجهول
		النهي	الأمر

d)

الاسم الفاعل	المصدر	المضارع المعروف	اصْفَرَّ
الاسم الفاعل	المصدر	المضارع المعروف	الماضي المعروف
الاسم المفعول	المصدر	المضارع المجهول	الماضي المجهول
		النهي	الأمر

e)

			ابْيَضَّ
الاسم الفاعل	المصدر	المضارع المعروف	الماضي المعروف
الاسم المفعول	المصدر	المضارع المجهول	الماضي المجهول
		النهي	الأمر

f)

			اغْبَرَّ
الاسم الفاعل	المصدر	المضارع المعروف	الماضي المعروف
الاسم المفعول	المصدر	المضارع المجهول	الماضي المجهول
		النهي	الأمر

Question 2: Please fill in the following:

al-Ifʿilāl al-Fiʿl al-Māḍī al-Muthbat al-Maʿrūf		
	Singular, male, third person	اسْوَدَّ
	Dual, male, third person	
	Plural, male, third person	
	Singular, female, third person	
	Dual, female, third person	
	Plural, female, third person	اسْوَدَدْنَ [5]
	Singular, male, second person	
	Dual, male, second person	
	Plural, male, second person	
	Singular, female, second person	
	Dual, female, second person	
	Plural, female second person	
	Singular, first person	
	Plural, first person	

---

[5] The rest of the pattern will be done in this manner. The two ٯ's will be separated with the second one being sākin.

al-Ifʿilāl al-Fiʿl al-Muḍāriʿ al-Manfī al-Maʿrūf

	Singular, male, third person	لَا يَغْبُرُ
	Dual, male, third person	
	Plural, male, third person	
	Singular, female, third person	
	Dual, female, third person	
	Plural, female, third person	لَا يَغْبَرْنَ
	Singular, male, second person	
	Dual, male, second person	
	Plural, male, second person	
	Singular, female, second person	
	Dual, female, second person	
	Plural, female second person	لَا تَغْبَرْنَ
	Singular, first person	
	Plural, first person	

al-Ifʿilāl al-Fiʿl al-Amr al-Maʿrūf		
	Singular, male, third person	لِيَصْفَرَّ
	Dual, male, third person	
	Plural, male, third person	
	Singular, female, third person	
	Dual, female, third person	
	Plural, female, third person	لِيَصْفَرَرْنَ
	Singular, male, second person	
	Dual, male, second person	
	Plural, male, second person	
	Singular, female, second person	
	Dual, female, second person	
	Plural, female second person	اصْفَرَرْنَ
	Singular, first person	
	Plural, first person	

Question 3: Translate the following into English:

وَإِذَا بُشِّرَ أَحَدُهُم بِالْأُنثَىٰ ظَلَّ وَجْهُهُ مُسْوَدًّا وَهُوَ كَظِيمٌ	(1
غَضِبَ حَتَّى احْمَرَّتْ وَجْنَتَاهُ	(2
ثُمَّ يَهِيجُ الزَّرْعُ فَتَرَاهُ مُصْفَرًّا	(3
كَنَسَتِ الْبَيْتَ حَتَّى اغْبَرَّتْ ثِيَابُهَا	(4
وَيَوْمَ الْقِيَامَةِ تَرَى الَّذِينَ كَذَبُوا عَلَى اللهِ وُجُوهُهُم مُسْوَدَّةٌ	(5

(6	قَالُوا: يَا رَسُولَ اللهِ قَحَطَ المَطَرُ، وَاحْمَرَّتِ الشَّجَرُ، وَهَلَكَتِ البَهَائِمُ
(7	فَإِذَا حَمْزَةُ قَدْ ثَمِلَ، مُحْمَرَّةً عَيْنَاهُ
(8	صَبَغَتْ فَاطِمَةُ شَعْرَهَا فَاشْقَرَّ
(9	وَلَوْ أَنَّ أُحُدًا ارْفَضَّ لِلَّذِي صَنَعْتُمْ بِعُثْمَانَ لَكَانَ مَحْقُوقًا أَنْ يَرْفَضَّ
(10	أَلَمْ تَرَ أَنَّ اللهَ أَنْزَلَ مِنَ السَّمَاءِ مَاءً فَتُصْبِحُ الْأَرْضُ مُخْضَرَّةً

11)	يَوْمَ تَبْيَضُّ وُجُوهٌ وَتَسْوَدُّ وُجُوهٌ
12)	حَبَسَ الْمُشْرِكُونَ رَسُولَ اللهِ صَلَّى اللهُ عَلَيْهِ وَسَلَّمَ عَنْ صَلَاةِ الْعَصْرِ حَتَّى احْمَرَّتِ الشَّمْسُ أَوِ اصْفَرَّتْ
13)	يَقَظَ النَّبِيُّ صَلَّى اللهُ عَلَيْهِ وَسَلَّمَ مِنَ النَّوْمِ مُحْمَرًّا وَجْهُهُ
14)	طُوبَى لِعَبْدٍ آخِذٍ بِعِنَانِ فَرَسِهِ فِي سَبِيلِ اللهِ، أَشْعَثَ رَأْسُهُ، مُغْبَرَّةٍ قَدَمَاهُ
15)	لَا يَزَالُ الْعَبْدُ يَكْذِبُ وَتُنْكَتُ فِي قَلْبِهِ نُكْتَةٌ سَوْدَاءُ حَتَّى يَسْوَدَّ قَلْبُهُ كُلُّهُ

Question 4: Fill out the following chart:

	Masdar	Verb Form		Arabic
1.	اسوداد	Amr Maʿrūf	Plural, first person	
	Translation			
2.	احمرار	Māḍī Muthbat Maʿrūf	Singular, first person	
	Translation			
3.	اخضرار	Muḍāriʿ Muthbat Maʿrūf	Singular, male, third person	
	Translation			
4.	ازرقاق	Māḍī Manfī Maʿrūf	Plural, male, second person	
	Translation			
5.	اسوداد	Nahī Maʿrūf	Dual, female, third person	
	Translation			

	Masdar	Verb Form		Arabic
6.	اشقرار	Ism Fāʿil	Plural, female	
	Translation			
7.	اصفرار	Amr Maʿrūf	Singular, male, second person	
	Translation			
8.	ابيضاض	Nahī Maʿrūf	Plural, first person	
	Translation			
9.	اسمرار	Muḍāriʿ Muthbat Maʿrūf	Plural, female, second person	
	Translation			
10.	اغبرار	Māḍī Manfī Maʿrūf	Dual, male	
	Translation			

Masdar	Verb Form		Arabic
11.			مُزْرَقَّانِ
Translation			
12.			لِتَشْقَرَّا
Translation			
13.			مُسْوَدُّونَ
Translation			
14.			مَا اصْفَرَّتَا
Translation			
15.			لَا أَبْيَضَّ
Translation			

Unit 10: The Tenth Pattern – استفعال

This pattern is identified by the number X in the Hans Wehr dictionary. This
pattern is often used to request something.

مُسْتَفْعِلٌ	اِسْتِفْعَالًا	يَسْتَفْعِلُ	اِسْتَفْعَلَ
الاسم الفاعل	المصدر	المضارع المعروف	الماضي المعروف
مُسْتَفْعَلٌ	اِسْتِفْعَالًا	يُسْتَفْعَلُ	أُسْتُفْعِلَ
الاسم المفعول	المصدر	المضارع المجهول	الماضي المجهول
		لَا تَسْتَفْعِلْ	اِسْتَفْعِلْ
		النهي	الأمر

Exercises

Question 1: Please fill in the following:

a)

			اخْمَرَّ
الاسم الفاعل	المصدر	المضارع المعروف	الماضي المعروف
الاسم المفعول	المصدر	المضارع المجهول	الماضي المجهول
		النهي	الأمر

b)

			اسْوَدَّ
الاسم الفاعل	المصدر	المضارع المعروف	الماضي المعروف
الاسم المفعول	المصدر	المضارع المجهول	الماضي المجهول
		النهي	الأمر

c)

			اخْضَرَّ
الاسم الفاعل	المصدر	المضارع المعروف	الماضي المعروف
الاسم المفعول	المصدر	المضارع المجهول	الماضي المجهول
		النهي	الأمر

d)

			اصْفَرَّ
الاسم الفاعل	المصدر	المضارع المعروف	الماضي المعروف
الاسم المفعول	المصدر	المضارع المجهول	الماضي المجهول
		النهي	الأمر

e)

			ابْيَضَّ
الاسم الفاعل	المصدر	المضارع المعروف	الماضي المعروف
الاسم المفعول	المصدر	المضارع المجهول	الماضي المجهول
		النهي	الأمر

f)

			اغْبَرَّ
الاسم الفاعل	المصدر	المضارع المعروف	الماضي المعروف
الاسم المفعول	المصدر	المضارع المجهول	الماضي المجهول
		النهي	الأمر

Question 2: Please fill in the following:

al-Istifʿāl al-Fiʿl al-Māḍī al-Muthbat al-Maʿrūf		
	Singular, male, third person	اسْتَكْبَرَ
	Dual, male, third person	
	Plural, male, third person	
	Singular, female, third person	
	Dual, female, third person	
	Plural, female, third person	
	Singular, male, second person	
	Dual, male, second person	
	Plural, male, second person	
	Singular, female, second person	
	Dual, female, second person	
	Plural, female second person	
	Singular, first person	
	Plural, first person	

al-Istifʿāl al-Fiʿl al-Muḍāriʿ al-Muthbat al-Maʿrūf		
	Singular, male, third person	يَسْتَمْتِعُ
	Dual, male, third person	
	Plural, male, third person	
	Singular, female, third person	
	Dual, female, third person	
	Plural, female, third person	
	Singular, male, second person	
	Dual, male, second person	
	Plural, male, second person	
	Singular, female, second person	
	Dual, female, second person	
	Plural, female second person	
	Singular, first person	
	Plural, first person	

al-Istifʿāl al-Fiʿl al-Muḍāriʿ al-Muthbat al-Majhūl		
	Singular, male, third person	يُسْتَغْفَرُ
	Dual, male, third person	
	Plural, male, third person	
	Singular, female, third person	
	Dual, female, third person	
	Plural, female, third person	
	Singular, male, second person	
	Dual, male, second person	
	Plural, male, second person	
	Singular, female, second person	
	Dual, female, second person	
	Plural, female second person	
	Singular, first person	
	Plural, first person	

145

	al-Istifʿāl al-Fiʿl al-Nahī al-Maʿrūf	
	Singular, male, third person	لَا يَسْتَفْسِرْ
	Dual, male, third person	
	Plural, male, third person	
	Singular, female, third person	
	Dual, female, third person	
	Plural, female, third person	
	Singular, male, second person	
	Dual, male, second person	
	Plural, male, second person	
	Singular, female, second person	
	Dual, female, second person	
	Plural, female second person	
	Singular, first person	
	Plural, first person	

Question 3: Translate the following into English:

قَالَ اللهُ سُبْحَانَهُ وَ تَعَالَى لِلشَّيْطَانِ وَاسْتَفْزِزْ بِصَوْتِكَ	(1
وَأَمَّا الَّذِينَ اسْتَنْكَفُوا وَاسْتَكْبَرُوا فَيُعَذِّبُهُمْ عَذَابًا أَلِيمًا	(2
وَمَا كَانَ اسْتِغْفَارُ إِبْرَاهِيمَ لِأَبِيهِ إِلَّا عَنْ مَوْعِدَةٍ وَعَدَهَا	(3
وَتَسْتَخْرِجُونَ حِلْيَةً تَلْبَسُونَهَا	(4
عَسَى رَبُّكُمْ أَنْ يُهْلِكَ عَدُوَّكُمْ وَيَسْتَخْلِفَكُمْ فِي الْأَرْضِ	(5

مَثَلُهُمْ كَمَثَلِ الَّذِي اسْتَوْقَدَ نَارًا	(6
كَانُوا مِنْ قَبْلُ يَسْتَفْتِحُونَ عَلَى الَّذِينَ كَفَرُوا	(7
كُنْتُمْ تَسْتَكْبِرُونَ فِي الْأَرْضِ بِغَيْرِ الْحَقِّ	(8
وَيَسْتَنْبِئُونَكَ أَحَقٌّ هُوَ قُلْ إِي وَرَبِّي إِنَّهُ لَحَقٌّ	(9
أَرَادَ رَبُّكَ أَنْ يَبْلُغَا أَشُدَّهُمَا وَيَسْتَخْرِجَا كَنْزَهُمَا	(10

لَا يَسْتَكْبِرُونَ عَنْ عِبَادَتِهِ وَلَا يَسْتَحْسِرُونَ _____	(11
قَالَ اللهُ: ثَلَاثَةٌ أَنَا خَصْمُهُمْ يَوْمَ الْقِيَامَةِ ... وَرَجُلٌ اسْتَأْجَرَ أَجِيرًا وَلَمْ يُعْطِ أَجْرَهُ _____ _____	(12
لَا يَسْتَأْذِنُكَ الَّذِينَ يُؤْمِنُونَ بِاللهِ وَالْيَوْمِ الْآخِرِ أَنْ يُجَاهِدُوا بِأَمْوَالِهِمْ وَأَنْفُسِهِمْ _____ _____	(13
كَأَنَّهُمْ حُمُرٌ مُسْتَنْفِرَةٌ _____ _____	(14
عَنْ عَلِيٍّ، أَنَّ فَاطِمَةَ، أَتَتِ النَّبِيَّ صَلَّى اللهُ عَلَيْهِ وَسَلَّمَ تَسْتَخْدِمُهُ، فَقَالَ: أَلَا أَدُلُّكِ عَلَى مَا هُوَ خَيْرٌ لَكِ مِنْ ذَلِكِ تُسَبِّحِينَ ثَلَاثًا وَثَلَاثِينَ، وَتُكَبِّرِينَ ثَلَاثًا وَثَلَاثِينَ، وَتُحَمِّدِينَ ثَلَاثًا وَثَلَاثِينَ _____ _____	(15

Question 4: Fill out the following chart:

	Masdar	Verb Form		Arabic
16.	استمساك	Ism Fāʿil	Plural, female	
	Translation			
17.	استعجال	Amr Maʿrūf	Singular, male, second person	
	Translation			
18.	استحلاف	Nahī Maʿrūf	Plural, first person	
	Translation			
19.	استغفار	Muḍāriʿ Muthbat Majhūl	Plural, female, second person	
	Translation			
20.	استنطاق	Māḍī Manfī Majhūl	Dual, male, third person	
	Translation			

	Masdar	Verb Form		Arabic
21.	استبشار	Ism Mafʿūl	Dual, male	
	Translation			
22.	استحضار	Amr Majhūl	Singular, male, third person	
	Translation			
23.	استسلام	Ism Fāʿil	Plural, male	
	Translation			
24.	استرحام	Māḍī Manfī Majhūl	Dual, female, third person	
	Translation			
25.	استخراج	Nahī Maʿrūf	Singular, first person	
	Translation			

	Masdar	Verb Form		Arabic
26.				لِنُسْتَصْغَرْ
	Translation			
27.				مُسْتَظْلَعَاتٌ
	Translation			
28.				تُسْتَعْمَلَانِ
	Translation			
29.				اسْتَقْدَمْتِ
	Translation			
30.				لِنَسْتَحْصِدْ
	Translation			

Review: Lessons 1-9

Question 1: Fill out the following charts using the root of the verb بَشَرَ.

باب التَّفْعِيْل			
الاسم الفاعل	المصدر	المضارع المعروف	الماضي المعروف
الاسم المفعول	المصدر	المضارع المجهول	الماضي المجهول
		النهي	الأمر

باب الْمُفَاعَلَة			
الاسم الفاعل	المصدر	المضارع المعروف	الماضي المعروف
الاسم المفعول	المصدر	المضارع المجهول	الماضي المجهول
		النهي	الأمر

باب الْإِفْعَال			
الاسم الفاعل	المصدر	المضارع المعروف	الماضي المعروف
الاسم المفعول	المصدر	المضارع المجهول	الماضي المجهول
		النهي	الأمر

			باب التَّفَعُّل
الاسم الفاعل	المصدر	المضارع المعروف	الماضي المعروف
الاسم المفعول	المصدر	المضارع المجهول	الماضي المجهول
		النهي	الأمر

			باب التَّفَاعُل
الاسم الفاعل	المصدر	المضارع المعروف	الماضي المعروف
الاسم المفعول	المصدر	المضارع المجهول	الماضي المجهول
		النهي	الأمر

			باب الْاِنْفِعَال
الاسم الفاعل	المصدر	المضارع المعروف	الماضي المعروف
الاسم المفعول	المصدر	المضارع المجهول	الماضي المجهول
		النهي	الأمر

باب الْافْتِعَال

الاسم الفاعل	المصدر	المضارع المعروف	الماضي المعروف
الاسم المفعول	المصدر	المضارع المجهول	الماضي المجهول
		النهي	الأمر

باب الْافْعِلَال

الاسم الفاعل	المصدر	المضارع المعروف	الماضي المعروف
الاسم المفعول	المصدر	المضارع المجهول	الماضي المجهول
		النهي	الأمر

باب الْاسْتِفْعَال

الاسم الفاعل	المصدر	المضارع المعروف	الماضي المعروف
الاسم المفعول	المصدر	المضارع المجهول	الماضي المجهول
		النهي	الأمر

Question 2: Please fill in the following using the root of the verb written in brackets:

باب الإسْتِفْعَال - Istif'āl al-Fi'l al-Māḍī al-Muthbat al-Majhūl (ذكر)		
	Singular, male, third person	
	Dual, male, third person	
	Plural, male, third person	
	Singular, female, third person	
	Dual, female, third person	
	Plural, female, third person	
	Singular, male, second person	
	Dual, male, second person	
	Plural, male, second person	
	Singular, female, second person	
	Dual, female, second person	
	Plural, female second person	
	Singular, first person	
	Plural, first person	

	al-Ifʿīlāl al-Fiʿl al-Māḍī al-Manfī al-Maʿrūf (حمر) - باب الإفْعِلَال	
	Singular, male, third person	
	Dual, male, third person	
	Plural, male, third person	
	Singular, female, third person	
	Dual, female, third person	
	Plural, female, third person	
	Singular, male, second person	
	Dual, male, second person	
	Plural, male, second person	
	Singular, female, second person	
	Dual, female, second person	
	Plural, female second person	
	Singular, first person	
	Plural, first person	

	al-Tafāʿul al-Fiʿl al-Muḍāriʿ al-Muthbat al-Maʿrūf (درك) - باب التَّفَاعُل	
	Singular, male, third person	
	Dual, male, third person	
	Plural, male, third person	
	Singular, female, third person	
	Dual, female, third person	
	Plural, female, third person	
	Singular, male, second person	
	Dual, male, second person	
	Plural, male, second person	
	Singular, female, second person	
	Dual, female, second person	
	Plural, female second person	
	Singular, first person	
	Plural, first person	

	al-Iftiʿāl al-Fiʿl al-Muḍāriʿ al-Manfī al-Majhūl (جنب) - باب الاِفْتِعَال	
	Singular, male, third person	
	Dual, male, third person	
	Plural, male, third person	
	Singular, female, third person	
	Dual, female, third person	
	Plural, female, third person	
	Singular, male, second person	
	Dual, male, second person	
	Plural, male, second person	
	Singular, female, second person	
	Dual, female, second person	
	Plural, female second person	
	Singular, first person	
	Plural, first person	

al-Mufāʿala al-Fiʿl al-Amr al-Maʿrūf (قتل) - باب المُفَاعَلَة		
	Singular, male, third person	
	Dual, male, third person	
	Plural, male, third person	
	Singular, female, third person	
	Dual, female, third person	
	Plural, female, third person	
	Singular, male, second person	
	Dual, male, second person	
	Plural, male, second person	
	Singular, female, second person	
	Dual, female, second person	
	Plural, female second person	
	Singular, first person	
	Plural, first person	

باب المُفَاعَلَة - al-Mufāʿala al-Fiʿl al-Amr al-Maʿrūf (قتل)

باب التَّفَعُّل - al-Tafaʿul al-Fiʿl al-Nahī al-Maʿrūf (حسن)		
	Singular, male, third person	
	Dual, male, third person	
	Plural, male, third person	
	Singular, female, third person	
	Dual, female, third person	
	Plural, female, third person	
	Singular, male, second person	
	Dual, male, second person	
	Plural, male, second person	
	Singular, female, second person	
	Dual, female, second person	
	Plural, female second person	
	Singular, first person	
	Plural, first person	

باب التَّفَعُّل - al-Tafaʿul al-Fiʿl al-Nahī al-Maʿrūf (حسن)

Question 3: Translate the following into English:

1)	مَنِ اغْبَرَّتْ قَدَمَاهُ فِي سَبِيلِ اللهِ حَرَّمَهُ اللهُ عَلَى النَّارِ _____ _____
2)	اسْتَحْوَذَ عَلَيْهِمُ الشَّيْطَانُ _____
3)	الْمَلَائِكَةُ يَجْتَمِعُونَ فِي صَلَاةِ الْفَجْرِ وَصَلَاةِ الْعَصْرِ _____ _____
4)	وَإِذَا قُرِئَ الْقُرْآنُ فَاسْتَمِعُوا لَهُ وَأَنْصِتُوا لَعَلَّكُمْ تُرْحَمُونَ _____ _____
5)	أَفَلَا تُبْصِرُونَ _____ _____

6)	يَخْرُجُ مِنْ بُطُونِ النَّحْلِ شَرَابٌ مُخْتَلِفٌ أَلْوَانُهُ فِيهِ شِفَاءٌ لِلنَّاسِ
7)	يَا أَيُّهَا الَّذِينَ آمَنُوا لَا تَدْخُلُوا بُيُوتًا غَيْرَ بُيُوتِكُمْ حَتَّى تَسْتَأْنِسُوا وَتُسَلِّمُوا عَلَى أَهْلِهَا
8)	اِرْفَضَّ الاجْتِمَاعُ
9)	الَّذِينَ مِنْ قَبْلِهِمْ كَذَّبُوا بِآيَاتِنَا
10)	غُفْرَانَكَ الْحَمْدُ لِلَّهِ الَّذِي أَذْهَبَ عَنِّي الْأَذَى وَعَافَانِي

11) قَالُوا ادْعُ لَنَا رَبَّكَ يُبَيِّنْ لَنَا مَا هِيَ إِنَّ الْبَقَرَ تَشَابَهَ عَلَيْنَا

_____

_____

12) مَا لَكُمْ لَا تَنَاصَرُونَ

_____

_____

13) سَابِقُوا إِلَى مَغْفِرَةٍ مِنْ رَبِّكُمْ وَجَنَّةٍ عَرْضُهَا كَعَرْضِ السَّمَاءِ وَالْأَرْضِ

_____

_____

14) وَإِذْ يَرْفَعُ إِبْرَاهِيمُ الْقَوَاعِدَ مِنَ الْبَيْتِ وَإِسْمَاعِيلُ رَبَّنَا تَقَبَّلْ مِنَّا

_____

_____

15) إِذَا صَلَّيْتُمْ فَلَا تَلْتَفِتُوا فِي صَلَاتِكُمْ

_____

_____

Question 4: Fill out the following chart:

	Masdar	Pattern	Verb Form		Arabic
1.	اشتداد		Ism Fāʿil	Dual, female	
2.	استغفار		Amr Majhūl	Singular, first person	
3.	افتراق		Nahī Majhūl	Singular, male, second person	
4.	تضاحك		Muḍāriʿ Muthbat Maʿrūf	Plural, first person	
5.	اشقرار		Māḍī Manfī Maʿrūf	Plural, female, third person	

	Masdar	Pattern	Verb Form		Arabic
6.	انكسار		Māḍī Manfī Maʿrūf	Dual, female, third person	
7.	اختصاص		Nahī Maʿrūf	Singular, first person	
8.	تذاكر		Amr Maʿrūf	Plural, first person	
9.	اسوداد		Ism Fāʿil	Plural, female	
10.	إفلاح		Muḍāriʿ Muthbat Maʿrūf	Singular, male, third person	

Masdar	Pattern	Verb Form		Arabic
11.				اقْتَرَبَتِ
12.				لِئُعَانَقْ
13.				مَا تَصَدَّقْتُمْ
14.				مَا انْتُصِرْتُمَا
15.				مُسْتَرْحَمُونَ

Rare Patterns

Appendix: Rare Patterns

As we learned previously, al-Thulāthī al-Mazīd Fīh (الثُّلَاثِيُّ الْمَزِيدُ فِيهِ) fiʿl is a fiʿl which is comprised of three root letters, and there are additional letters joined to them in its Māḍī form.

Example: أَرْسَلَ: He sent

There are 14 patterns of al-Thulāthī al-Mazīd Fīh in total. The first 9 patterns which were previously covered are the commonly used ones. The remaining 5 are rarely used.

The 5 rarely used patterns are:

بَاب الِافْعِيلَال	اِفْعَالَّ يَفْعَالُّ – افْعِيلَالًا	(1
بَاب الِافْعِيعَال	اِفْعَوْعَلَ يَفْعَوْعِلُ – افْعِيعَالًا	(2
بَاب الِافَّاعُل	اِفَّاعَلَ يَفَّاعَلُ – اِفَّاعُلًا	(3
بَاب الِافَّعُّل	اِفَّعَّلَ يَفَّعَّلُ – اِفَّعُّلًا	(4
بَاب الِافْعِوَّال	اِفْعَوَّلَ يَفْعَوِّلُ – اِفْعِوَّالًا	(5

Unit 11: The Eleventh Pattern – الافعيلال

This pattern is always Lāzim which means that it does not get majhūl verbs, mafʿūl bihīs and ism mafʿūls. This pattern is often used to express colours and flaws.

مُفْعَالٌّ	افْعِيلَالًا	يَفْعَالُّ	إِفْعَالَّ
الاسم الفاعل	المصدر	المضارع المعروف	الماضي المعروف
---	---	---	---
الاسم المفعول	المصدر	المضارع المجهول	الماضي المجهول
		لَا تَفْعَالَّ	إِفْعَالَّ
		النهي	الأمر

Exercises

Question 1: Please fill in the following:

a)

			اذْهامَّ
الاسم الفاعل	المصدر	المضارع المعروف	الماضي المعروف
الاسم المفعول	المصدر	المضارع المجهول	الماضي المجهول
		النهي	الأمر

b)

			اسْمارَّ
الاسم الفاعل	المصدر	المضارع المعروف	الماضي المعروف
الاسم المفعول	المصدر	المضارع المجهول	الماضي المجهول
		النهي	الأمر

c)

			اكْماتَّ
الاسم الفاعل	المصدر	المضارع المعروف	الماضي المعروف
الاسم المفعول	المصدر	المضارع المجهول	الماضي المجهول
		النهي	الأمر

Unit 12: The Twelfth Pattern – الافعيعال

This pattern is always Lāzim which means that it does not get majhūl verbs, mafʿūl bihīs and ism mafʿūls.

مُفْعَوْعِلٌ	اِفْعِيعَالًا	يَفْعَوْعِلُ	اِفْعَوْعَلَ
الاسم الفاعل	المصدر	المضارع المعروف	الماضي المعروف
---	---	---	---
الاسم المفعول	المصدر	المضارع المجهول	الماضي المجهول
	لَا تَفْعَوْعِلْ		اِفْعَوْعِلْ
	النهي		الأمر

Exercises

Question 1: Please fill in the following:

a)

			اخْشَوْشَنَ
الاسم الفاعل	المصدر	المضارع المعروف	الماضي المعروف
الاسم المفعول	المصدر	المضارع المجهول	الماضي المجهول
الأمر		النهي	

b)

			امْلَوْلَحَ
الاسم الفاعل	المصدر	المضارع المعروف	الماضي المعروف
الاسم المفعول	المصدر	المضارع المجهول	الماضي المجهول
الأمر		النهي	

c)

			احْدَوْدَبَ
الاسم الفاعل	المصدر	المضارع المعروف	الماضي المعروف
الاسم المفعول	المصدر	المضارع المجهول	الماضي المجهول
الأمر		النهي	

Unit 13: The Thirteenth Pattern – الافَاعُل

This pattern is always Lāzim which means that it does not get majhūl verbs, mafʿūl bihīs and ism mafʿūls.

مُفَّاعِلًا	إفَّاعُلًا	يَفَّاعَلُ	إفَّاعَلَ
الاسم الفاعل	المصدر	المضارع المعروف	الماضي المعروف
---	---	---	---
الاسم المفعول	المصدر	المضارع المجهول	الماضي المجهول
		لَا تَفَّاعَلْ	إفَّاعَلْ
		النهي	الأمر

Exercises

Question 1: Please fill in the following:

a)

			اسَّاقَطَ
الاسم الفاعل	المصدر	المضارع المعروف	الماضي المعروف
الاسم المفعول	المصدر	المضارع المجهول	الماضي المجهول
		النهي	الأمر

b)

			اشَّابَهَ
الاسم الفاعل	المصدر	المضارع المعروف	الماضي المعروف
الاسم المفعول	المصدر	المضارع المجهول	الماضي المجهول
		النهي	الأمر

c)

			اصَّالَحَ
الاسم الفاعل	المصدر	المضارع المعروف	الماضي المعروف
الاسم المفعول	المصدر	المضارع المجهول	الماضي المجهول
		النهي	الأمر

Unit 14: The Fourteenth Pattern – الافْعَلَّ

This pattern is always Lāzim which means that it does not get majhūl verbs, mafʿūl bihīs and ism mafʿūls.

مُفْعَلًّا	اِفْعَلًّا	يَفْعَلُّ	اِفْعَلَّ
الاسم الفاعل	المصدر	المضارع المعروف	الماضي المعروف
---	---	---	---
الاسم المفعول	المصدر	المضارع المجهول	الماضي المجهول
		لَا تَفْعَلَّ	اِفْعَلَّ
		النهي	الأمر

Exercises

Question 1: Please fill in the following:

a)

			ازَّمَّلَ
الاسم الفاعل	المصدر	المضارع المعروف	الماضي المعروف
الاسم المفعول	المصدر	المضارع المجهول	الماضي المجهول
		النهي	الأمر

b)

			اضَّرَّعَ
الاسم الفاعل	المصدر	المضارع المعروف	الماضي المعروف
الاسم المفعول	المصدر	المضارع المجهول	الماضي المجهول
		النهي	الأمر

c)

			اذَّكَّرَ
الاسم الفاعل	المصدر	المضارع المعروف	الماضي المعروف
الاسم المفعول	المصدر	المضارع المجهول	الماضي المجهول
		النهي	الأمر

Unit 15: The Fifteenth Pattern – الْإِفْعِوَّال

This pattern is always Lāzim which means that it does not get majhūl verbs, mafʿūl bihīs and ism mafʿūls.

مُفْعَوَّلٌ	اِفْعِوَّالًا	يَفْعَوَّلُ	اِفْعَوَّلَ
الاسم الفاعل	المصدر	المضارع المعروف	الماضي المعروف
---	---	---	---
الاسم المفعول	المصدر	المضارع المجهول	الماضي المجهول
	لَا تَفْعَوَّلْ		اِفْعَوَّلْ
	النهي		الأمر

Exercises

Question 1: Please fill in the following:

a)

			اجْلَوَّذَ
الاسم الفاعل	المصدر	المضارع المعروف	الماضي المعروف
الاسم المفعول	المصدر	المضارع المجهول	الماضي المجهول
		النهي	الأمر

b)

			اعْلَوَّطَ
الاسم الفاعل	المصدر	المضارع المعروف	الماضي المعروف
الاسم المفعول	المصدر	المضارع المجهول	الماضي المجهول
		النهي	الأمر

c)

			اخْرَوَّطَ
الاسم الفاعل	المصدر	المضارع المعروف	الماضي المعروف
الاسم المفعول	المصدر	المضارع المجهول	الماضي المجهول
		النهي	الأمر

Final Review

Question 1: Fill out the following charts using the root of the verb ضَرَبَ

			باب التَّفْعِيْل
الاسم الفاعل	المصدر	المضارع المعروف	الماضي المعروف
الاسم المفعول	المصدر	المضارع المجهول	الماضي المجهول
		النهي	الأمر

			باب الْمُفَاعَلَة
الاسم الفاعل	المصدر	المضارع المعروف	الماضي المعروف
الاسم المفعول	المصدر	المضارع المجهول	الماضي المجهول
		النهي	الأمر

			باب الْإِفْعَال
الاسم الفاعل	المصدر	المضارع المعروف	الماضي المعروف
الاسم المفعول	المصدر	المضارع المجهول	الماضي المجهول
		النهي	الأمر

باب التَّفَعُّل

الاسم الفاعل	المصدر	المضارع المعروف	الماضي المعروف
الاسم المفعول	المصدر	المضارع المجهول	الماضي المجهول
		النهي	الأمر

باب التَّفَاعُل

الاسم الفاعل	المصدر	المضارع المعروف	الماضي المعروف
الاسم المفعول	المصدر	المضارع المجهول	الماضي المجهول
		النهي	الأمر

باب الْإِنْفِعَال

الاسم الفاعل	المصدر	المضارع المعروف	الماضي المعروف
الاسم المفعول	المصدر	المضارع المجهول	الماضي المجهول
		النهي	الأمر

			باب الْاِفْتِعَال
الاسم الفاعل	المصدر	المضارع المعروف	الماضي المعروف
الاسم المفعول	المصدر	المضارع المجهول	الماضي المجهول
		النهي	الأمر

			باب الْاِفْعِلَال
الاسم الفاعل	المصدر	المضارع المعروف	الماضي المعروف
الاسم المفعول	المصدر	المضارع المجهول	الماضي المجهول
		النهي	الأمر

			باب الْاِسْتِفْعَال
الاسم الفاعل	المصدر	المضارع المعروف	الماضي المعروف
الاسم المفعول	المصدر	المضارع المجهول	الماضي المجهول
		النهي	الأمر

باب الْاِفْعِيلَال				
الاسم الفاعل	المصدر	المضارع المعروف	الماضي المعروف
الاسم المفعول	المصدر	المضارع المجهول	الماضي المجهول
		النهي	الأمر

باب الْاِفْعِيعَال				
الاسم الفاعل	المصدر	المضارع المعروف	الماضي المعروف
الاسم المفعول	المصدر	المضارع المجهول	الماضي المجهول
		النهي	الأمر

باب الْاِفَّاعُل				
الاسم الفاعل	المصدر	المضارع المعروف	الماضي المعروف
الاسم المفعول	المصدر	المضارع المجهول	الماضي المجهول
		النهي	الأمر

			باب الْاِفَّعُّل
الاسم الفاعل	المصدر	المضارع المعروف	الماضي المعروف
الاسم المفعول	المصدر	المضارع المجهول	الماضي المجهول
		النهي	الأمر

			باب الْاِفْعِوَّال
الاسم الفاعل	المصدر	المضارع المعروف	الماضي المعروف
الاسم المفعول	المصدر	المضارع المجهول	الماضي المجهول
		النهي	الأمر

Question 2: Please fill in the following using the root of the verb written in brackets:

	al-Fiʿl al-Māḍī al-Muthbat al-Maʿrūf (يسر) باب التَّفْعِيل	
	Singular, male, third person	
	Dual, male, third person	
	Plural, male, third person	
	Singular, female, third person	
	Dual, female, third person	
	Plural, female, third person	
	Singular, male, second person	
	Dual, male, second person	
	Plural, male, second person	
	Singular, female, second person	
	Dual, female, second person	
	Plural, female second person	
	Singular, first person	
	Plural, first person	

al- Mufāʿala al-Fiʿl al-Māḍī al-Muthbat al-Majhūl (شرك) – باب المُفاعَلَة		
	Singular, male, third person	
	Dual, male, third person	
	Plural, male, third person	
	Singular, female, third person	
	Dual, female, third person	
	Plural, female, third person	
	Singular, male, second person	
	Dual, male, second person	
	Plural, male, second person	
	Singular, female, second person	
	Dual, female, second person	
	Plural, female second person	
	Singular, first person	
	Plural, first person	

al- Mufāʿala al-Fiʿl al-Māḍī al-Muthbat al-Majhūl (شرك) – باب المُفاعَلَة

al-Ifʿāl al-Fiʿl al-Muḍāriʿ al-Muthbat al-Maʿrūf (رشد) - باب الإفْعَال		
	Singular, male, third person	
	Dual, male, third person	
	Plural, male, third person	
	Singular, female, third person	
	Dual, female, third person	
	Plural, female, third person	
	Singular, male, second person	
	Dual, male, second person	
	Plural, male, second person	
	Singular, female, second person	
	Dual, female, second person	
	Plural, female second person	
	Singular, first person	
	Plural, first person	

	Singular, male, third person	
	Dual, male, third person	
	Plural, male, third person	
	Singular, female, third person	
	Dual, female, third person	
	Plural, female, third person	
	Singular, male, second person	
	Dual, male, second person	
	Plural, male, second person	
	Singular, female, second person	
	Dual, female, second person	
	Plural, female second person	
	Singular, first person	
	Plural, first person	

al-Tafaʿul al-Fiʿl al-Muḍāriʿ al-Manfī al-Majhūl (دبر) - باب التَّفَعُّل

al-Tafāʿul al-Fiʿl al-Amr al-Maʿrūf (سمح) - باب التَّفَاعُل		
	Singular, male, third person	
	Dual, male, third person	
	Plural, male, third person	
	Singular, female, third person	
	Dual, female, third person	
	Plural, female, third person	
	Singular, male, second person	
	Dual, male, second person	
	Plural, male, second person	
	Singular, female, second person	
	Dual, female, second person	
	Plural, female second person	
	Singular, first person	
	Plural, first person	

al-Infiʿāl al-Fiʿl al-Māḍī al-Muthbat al-Maʿrūf (كسر) – باب الاِنْفِعَال		
	Singular, male, third person	
	Dual, male, third person	
	Plural, male, third person	
	Singular, female, third person	
	Dual, female, third person	
	Plural, female, third person	
	Singular, male, second person	
	Dual, male, second person	
	Plural, male, second person	
	Singular, female, second person	
	Dual, female, second person	
	Plural, female second person	
	Singular, first person	
	Plural, first person	

(كسب) الِافْتِعَال - al-Iftiʿāl al-Fiʿl al-Māḍī al-Muthbat al-Majhūl		
	Singular, male, third person	
	Dual, male, third person	
	Plural, male, third person	
	Singular, female, third person	
	Dual, female, third person	
	Plural, female, third person	
	Singular, male, second person	
	Dual, male, second person	
	Plural, male, second person	
	Singular, female, second person	
	Dual, female, second person	
	Plural, female second person	
	Singular, first person	
	Plural, first person	

الِافْتِعَال - al-Iftiʿāl al-Fiʿl al-Māḍī al-Muthbat al-Majhūl (كسب)

	al-Ifʿilāl al-Fiʿl al-Muḍāriʿ al-Muthbat al-Maʿrūf (سود) - باب الإفْعِلَال	
	Singular, male, third person	
	Dual, male, third person	
	Plural, male, third person	
	Singular, female, third person	
	Dual, female, third person	
	Plural, female, third person	
	Singular, male, second person	
	Dual, male, second person	
	Plural, male, second person	
	Singular, female, second person	
	Dual, female, second person	
	Plural, female second person	
	Singular, first person	
	Plural, first person	

	Singular, male, third person	
	Dual, male, third person	
	Plural, male, third person	
	Singular, female, third person	
	Dual, female, third person	
	Plural, female, third person	
	Singular, male, second person	
	Dual, male, second person	
	Plural, male, second person	
	Singular, female, second person	
	Dual, female, second person	
	Plural, female second person	
	Singular, first person	
	Plural, first person	

al-Istifʿāl al-Fiʿl al-Muḍāriʿ al-Manfī al-Majhūl (سمع) باب الاِسْتِفْعَال

باب الاِسْتِفْعَال - al-Istifʿāl al-Fiʿl al-Muḍāriʿ al-Manfī al-Majhūl (سمع)

Question 3: Translate the following into English:

لَا يَسْمَعُونَ فِيهَا لَغْوًا وَلَا تَأْثِيمًا	(1
لَا تُبَاشِرُوهُنَّ وَأَنْتُمْ عَاكِفُونَ فِي الْمَسَاجِدِ	(2
فَقُلْ أَسْلَمْتُ وَجْهِيَ لِلَّهِ	(3
وَمَن يَتَوَكَّلْ عَلَى اللهِ فَهُوَ حَسْبُهُ	(4
أُولَٰئِكَ الْمُقَرَّبُونَ	(5

(6	يَطُوفُ عَلَيْهِمْ وِلْدَانٌ مُخَلَّدُونَ
(7	إِنَّ اللهَ سَيُبْطِلُهُ
(8	وَإِذَا مَا أُنْزِلَتْ سُورَةٌ نَظَرَ بَعْضُهُمْ إِلَى بَعْضٍ هَلْ يَرَاكُمْ مِنْ أَحَدٍ ثُمَّ انْصَرَفُوا
(9	إِذَا ذَكَرُوا اللهَ فَاسْتَغْفَرُوا لِذُنُوبِهِمْ
(10	وَعَلَى اللهِ فَلْيَتَوَكَّلِ الْمُتَوَكِّلُونَ

وَأَنْهَارٌ مِّن لَّبَنٍ لَّمْ يَتَغَيَّرْ طَعْمُهُ	(11
عَاشِرُوهُنَّ بِالْمَعْرُوفِ	(12
إِنَّ فِي خَلْقِ السَّمَاوَاتِ وَالْأَرْضِ وَاخْتِلَافِ اللَّيْلِ وَالنَّهَارِ لَآيَاتٍ لِّأُولِي الْأَلْبَابِ	(13
اغْتَبَطَ التَّلَامِيذُ بِيَوْمِ الْعُطْلَةِ	(14
إِذْ قُلْنَا لِلْمَلَائِكَةِ اسْجُدُوا لِآدَمَ فَسَجَدُوا إِلَّا إِبْلِيسَ اسْتَكْبَرَ وَكَانَ مِنَ الْكَافِرِينَ	(15

إِنَّ الَّذِينَ آمَنُوا وَالَّذِينَ هَاجَرُوا وَجَاهَدُوا فِي سَبِيلِ اللهِ _____ _____ _____	16)
صِيَامُ شَهْرَيْنِ مُتَتَابِعَيْنِ _____	17)
انْفَلَقَ الْقَمَرُ عَلَى عَهْدِ رَسُولِ اللهِ صَلَّى اللهُ عَلَيْهِ وَسَلَّمَ _____ _____ _____	18)
اسْتَحْضَرَ الْقَاضِي الشَّاهِدَ _____	19)
نَزَّلَ عَلَيْكَ الْكِتَابَ بِالْحَقِّ مُصَدِّقًا لِمَا بَيْنَ يَدَيْهِ _____ _____	20)

Question 4: Fill out the following chart:

	Masdar	Pattern	Verb Form		Arabic
1.	استحضار		Nahī Maʿrūf	Singular, first person	
2.	تسائل		Amr Maʿrūf	Plural, first person	
3.	إحكام		Ism Mafʿūl	Plural, female	
4.	تأجيل		Muḍāriʿ Muthbat Majhūl	Dual, male, third person	
5.	توكُّل		Māḍī Muthbat Maʿrūf	Singular, female, second person	

	Masdar	Pattern	Verb Form		Arabic
6.	معاشرة		Amr Majhūl	Plural, first person	
7.	تخليد		Māḍī Manfī Majhūl	Plural, male, second person	
8.	انصراف		Māḍī Muthbat Maʿrūf	Dual, male, second person	
9.	اخْشِيشانَ		Ism Fāʿil	Plural, male	
10.	احمرار		Ism Fāʿil	Singular, female	

	Masdar	Pattern	Verb Form		Arabic
11.					مَا أَفْطَرْتُمَا
12.					لَا يَذَّكَّرُ
13.					اَزَّمَّلْتِ
14.					أَجْلَوَّذَ
15.					تَدْهَامِّيْنَ

Made in United States
Troutdale, OR
12/05/2023